Other Books by Mary Oliver

POETRY

No Voyage and Other Poems

The River Styx, Ohio, and Other Poems

Twelve Moons

American Primitive

Dream Work

House of Light

New and Selected Poems

White Pine

West Wind

CHAPBOOKS

The Night Traveler

Sleeping in the Forest

PROSE

A Poetry Handbook

Blue Pastures

Rules for the Dance

Winter Hours

PROSE, PROSE POEMS, AND POEMS

Mary Oliver

Houghton Mifflin Company

BOSTON   NEW YORK

1999

Library of Congress Cataloging-in-Publication Data

Oliver, Mary, date.
Winter hours : prose, prose poems, and poems / Mary Oliver.
p. cm.
ISBN 0-395-85084-3
I. Title.
PS3565.L5W56   1999   811'.54 — DC21   99-19141   CIP

Book design by Anne Chalmers
Typeface: Adobe Garamond

Printed in the United States of America

QUM 10 9 8 7 6 5 4 3 2 1

The drawing of Shelley's boat, used here on the cover and title page, is redrawn from
a sketch made by Shelley's friend and sailing companion Edward Williams. It is from
Maria Gisborne & Edward E. Williams: Shelley's Friends, Their Journals and Letters, ed.
Frederick L. Jones (Norman, Okla.: University of Oklahoma Press, 1951).

"I will not knowingly tell you a single untruth."

—Ywain the Knight of the Lion

Foreword

Reader, you may call what follows a collection of essays. I have in enough instances, though not in every instance, attempted to surround and surmount a subject, as it is said a proper essay should do. Whether I have done so with sufficient distinction, you may decide. The truth is that I was not holding the essay in mind, not exactly. I was thinking rather of Samuel Johnson's kind of "writing" — I don't mean his persuasions and logics, but his ruminations and conversations, which are so informed and lively, and kindly even in their wit, and which are built always upon the bedrock of his devotion to civilized life as they expand, as they are lit by his pointed and delicious waggery. It cannot be a fault, I am sure, to have taken such elevation as a model. Nor do I mean, by exposing it, to imply success, but only to reveal the ambition that fueled me.

Everything in this book is true, in the autobiographical sense of the word. That is, I have not written here out of imagination and invention, but out of meditation and memory. No doubt my memory has the usual partiality of the individual, and is not entirely trustworthy. Still, I have been loyal here to the experiences of my own life and not, as is required in the more designed arts, to the needs of the line or the paragraph.

I have felt all my life that I was wise, and tasteful too, to speak very little about myself—to deflect the curiosity in the personal self that descends upon writers, especially in this country and at this time, from both casual and avid readers. My feelings have changed, to some degree anyway. I am now neither a young writer nor a middle-aged writer but whatever comes next —although, surely, I am not yet old! I have published books for more than thirty-five years and written longer than that, and my work has found readers enough to create a small but persistent interest in my actual life.

Therefore I find a compelling reason to write something revealing, a little, my private and natural self—to offer something that must in the future be taken into consideration by any who would claim to know me. I am only too aware of the ways in which inclination and supposition will fill whatever spaces in this world, or a life, are left vacant. And so I say again: I myself am the author of this document; it has no other formal persona, as my books of poems certainly do.

Neither are these writings of event or of periods of time exactly, but created out of mood, of reaction to various happenings in the world, and of my own searchings and findings in, if you will allow it, the fields of the spirit. Not that the flesh here does not also sing in its human house; there is that too.

But don't look for a portrait that is chronological, or talks much about my professional life, or opens to public view the important and proper secrets of a heart. Consider what is written rather as parts of a conversation, or a long and slowly arriving letter—somewhat disorderly, natural in expression, and happily unfinished.

.   .   .

Poe, Frost, Hopkins, and Whitman were subjects of interest in classes I recently taught at Bennington College, in Vermont, where I now live part of each year.

Contents

Essays and Poems

Building the House

I KNOW A YOUNG MAN who can build almost anything
—a boat, a fence, kitchen cabinets, a table, a barn, a house.
And so serenely, and in so assured and right a manner, that it is
joy to watch him. All the same, what he seems to care for
best—what he seems positively to desire—is the hour of in-
terruption, of hammerless quiet, in which he will sit and write
down poems or stories that have come into his mind with clam-
bering and colorful force. Truly he is not very good at the puz-
zle of words—not nearly as good as he is with the mallet and
the measuring tape—but this in no way lessens his pleasure.
Moreover, he is in no hurry. Everything he learned, he learned
at a careful pace—will not the use of words come easier at last,
though he begin at the slowest trot? Also, in these intervals, he
is happy. In building things, he is his familiar self, which he
does not overvalue. But in the act of writing he is a grander
man, a surprise to us, and even more to himself. He is beyond
what he believed himself to be.

I understand his pleasure. I also know the enclosure of my
skills, and am no less pert than he when some flow takes me
over the edge of it. Usually, as it happens, this is toward the
work in which he is so capable. There appears in my mind a
form; I imagine it from boards of a certain breadth and length,

and nails, and all in cheerful response to some need I have or think I have, aligned with a space I see as opportunistic. I would not pry my own tooth, or cobble my own shoes, but I deliberate unfazed the niceties of woodworking — nothing, all my life, has checked me. At my side at this moment is a small table with one leg turned in slightly. For I have never at all built anything perfectly, or even very well, in spite of the pleasure such labor gives me. Nor am I done yet, though time has brought obstacles and spread them before me — a stiffness of the fingers, a refusal of the eyes to switch easily from near to far, or rather from far to near, and thus to follow the aim of the hammer toward the nail head, which yearly grows smaller, and smaller.

Once, in fact, I built a house. It was a minuscule house, a one-room, one-floored affair set in the ivies and vincas of the backyard, and made almost entirely of salvaged materials. Still, it had a door. And four windows. And, miraculously, a peaked roof, so I could stand easily inside, and walk around. After it was done, and a door hung, I strung a line from the house so that I could set a lamp upon the built-in table, under one of the windows. Across the yard, in the evening with the lamplight shining outward, it looked very sweet, and it gave me much satisfaction. It seemed a thing of great accomplishment, as indeed, for me, it was. It was the house I had built. There would be no other.

The labor of writing poems, of working with thought and emotion in the encasement (or is it the wings?) of language, is strange to nature, for we are first of all creatures of motion. Only secondly — only oddly, and not naturally, at moments of contemplation, joy, grief, prayer, or terror — are we found, while awake, in the posture of deliberate or hapless inaction. But such is the posture of the poet, poor laborer. The dancer dances, the painter dips and lifts and lays on the oils; the composer reaches at least across the octaves. The poet sits. The architect draws and measures, and travels to the quarry to tramp among the gleaming stones. The poet sits, or, if it is a fluid moment, he scribbles some words upon the page. The body, under this pressure of non-existing, begins to draw up like a muscle, and complain. An unsolvable disharmony of such work—the mind so hotly fired and the body so long quiescent—will come sooner or later to revolution, will demand action! For many years, in a place I called Blackwater Woods, I wrote while I walked. That motion, hardly more than a dreamy sauntering, worked for me; it kept my body happy while I scribbled. But sometimes it wasn't at all enough. I wanted to build, in the other way, with the teeth of the saw, and the explosions of the hammer, and the little shrieks of the screws winding down into their perfect nests.

2

I began the house when I returned one spring after a year of teaching in a midwestern city. I had been, for months, responsible, sedate, thoughtful, and, for most of my daylight hours, indoors. I was sick for activity. And so, instead of lingering on the porch with my arrangement of tools, banging and punching together some simple and useful thing—another bookshelf, another table—I began the house.

When anything is built in our town, it is more importantly a foundation than a structure. Nothing—be it ugly, nonconforming, in violation of bylaws or neighbors' rights—nothing, once up, has ever been torn down. And almost nothing exists as it was originally constructed. On our narrow strip of land we are a build-up, add-on society. My house today, crooked as it is, stands. It has an undeniable value: it exists. It may therefore be enlarged eventually, even unto rentable proportions. The present owners of the property would not dream of discarding it. I can see from the road, they have given it a new roof and straightened out some doubtful portions of the peaked section. To one end of the peak, they have attached a metal rod that holds, in the air above the house, a statue of a heron, in the attitude of easy flight. My little house, looking upward, must be astonished.

The tools I used in my building of the house, and in all my labor of this sort, were a motley assortment of hand tools: hammer, tack hammer, drivers of screws, rasps, planes, saws small-toothed and rip, pliers, wrenches, awls. They had once belonged to my grandfather, and some of them to my great-grandfather, who was a carpenter of quality, and used the finer title cabinet-maker. This man I know only from photographs and an odd story or two: for example, he built his own coffin, of walnut, and left it, to be ready when needed, with the town mortician. Eventually, like the tiniest of houses, and with his body inside, it was consumed by flame.

These tools, though so closely mine, were not made therefore easy for me to use. I was, frankly, accident-prone; while I was making anything my hands and shins and elbows, if not other parts of my body, were streaked with dirt and nicks.

Gusto, not finesse, was my trademark here. And often enough, with these tools, I would come to a place where I could not wrest some necessary motion from my own wrists, or lift, or cut through. Then I would have to wait, in frustration, for a friend or acquaintance, or even a stranger—male, and stronger than I—to come along, and I would simply ask for help to get past that instant, that twist of the screw. Provincetown men, though they may seem rough to the unknowing, are as delicious and courteous as men are made. "Sure, darling," the plumber would say, or the neighbor passing by, or the fisherman stepping over from his yard, and he would help me, and would make a small thing of it.

3

Whatever a house is to the heart and body of man—refuge, comfort, luxury—surely it is as much or more to the spirit. Think how often our dreams take place inside the houses of our imaginations! Sometimes these are fearful, gloomy, enclosed places. At other times they are bright and have many windows and are surrounded by gardens combed and invitational, or un-pathed and wild. Surely such houses appearing in our sleep-work represent the state of the soul, or, if you prefer it, the state of the mind. Real estate, in any case, is not the issue of dreams. The condition of our true and private self is what dreams are about. If you rise refreshed from a dream—a night's settlement inside some house that has filled you with pleasure—you are doing okay. If you wake to the memory of squeezing confinement, rooms without air or light, a door difficult or impossible to open, a troubling disorganization or even wreckage inside, you are in trouble—with yourself. There are (dream) houses that pin themselves upon the windy porches of mountains, that open their own windows and summon in flocks of wild and colorful birds—and there are houses that hunker upon narrow ice floes adrift upon endless, dark waters; houses that creak, houses that sing; houses that will say nothing at all to you though you beg and plead all night for some answer to your vexing questions.

As such houses in dreams are mirrors of the mind or the soul, so an actual house, such as I began to build, is at least a little of that inner state made manifest. Jung, in a difficult time, slowly built a stone garden and a stone tower. Thoreau's house at Walden Pond, ten feet by fifteen feet under the tall, arrowy pines, was surely a dream-shape come to life. For anyone, stepping away from actions where one knows one's measure is good. It shakes away an excess of seriousness. Building my house, or anything else, I always felt myself becoming, in an almost devotional sense, passive, and willing to play. Play is never far from the impress of the creative drive, never far from the happiness of discovery. Building my house, I was joyous all day long.

The material issue of a house, however, is a matter not so much of imagination and spirit as it is of particular, joinable, weighty substance—it is brick and wood, it is foundation and beam, sash and sill; it is threshold and door and the latch upon the door. In the seventies and the eighties, in this part of the world if not everywhere, there was an ongoing, monstrous binge of building, or tearing back and rebuilding—and carting away of old materials to the (then-titled) dump. Which, in those days, was a lively and even social place. Work crews made a continual effort toward bulldozing the droppings from the trucks into some sort of order, shoving at least a dozen categories of broken and forsaken materials, along with reusable materials, into separate areas. Gulls, in flocks like low, white clouds, screamed and rippled over the heaps of lumber, looking for garbage that was also dumped, and often in no particular area. Motels, redecorating, would bring three hundred mattresses in the morning, three hundred desks in the afternoon. Treasures, of course, were abundantly sought and found. And good wood—useful wood—wood it was a sin to bury, not to use again. The price of lumber had not yet skyrocketed, so even new lumber lay seamed in with the old, the price passed on to the customer. Cut-offs, and lengths. Pine, fir, oak flooring, shingles of red and white cedar, ply, cherry trim, also tarpaper and insulation, screen doors new and old, and stovepipe old and new, and bricks, and, more than once, some power tools left carelessly, I suppose, in a truck bed, under the heaps of trash. This is where I went for my materials, along with others, men and women both, who simply roved, attentively, through all the mess until they found what they needed, or felt they would, someday, use. Clothes, furniture, old dolls, old highchairs, bikes; once a child's metal bank in the shape of a dog, very old; once a set of copper-bottomed cookware still in its original cartons; once a bag of old Christmas cards swept from the house of a man who had died only a month or so earlier, in almost every one of them a dollar bill.

Here I found everything I needed, including nails from half-full boxes spilled into the sand. All I lacked—only because

I lacked the patience to wait until it came along—was one of the ridge beams; this I bought at the local lumber company and paid cash for; thus the entire house cost me $3.58.

Oh, the intimidating and beautiful hardwoods! No more could I cut across the cherry or walnut or the oak than across stone! It was pine I looked for, with its tawny pattern of rings, its crisp knots, its willingness to be broken, cut, split, and its fragrance that never reached the air but made the heart gasp with its sweetness. Plywood I had no love of, though I took it when found and used it when I could, knowing it was no real thing, and alien to the weather, and apt to parch and swell, or buckle, or rot. Still, I used it. My little house was a patchwork. It was organic as a garden. It was free of any promise of exact inches, though at last it achieved a fair if not a strict linearity. On its foundation of old railroad ties, its framing of old wood, old ply, its sheets of tarpaper, its rows of pale shingles, it stood up. Stemming together everything with sixpenny nails, eight-penny nails, spikes, screws, I was involved, frustrated, devoted, resolved, nicked and scraped, and delighted. The work went slowly. The roof went on, was shingled with red cedar. I was a poet, but I was away for a while from the loom of thought and formal language; I was playing. I was whimsical, absorbed, happy. Let me always be who I am, and then some.

When my house was finished, my friend Stanley Kunitz gave me a yellow door, discarded from his house at the other end of town. Inside, I tacked up a van Gogh landscape, a Blake poem, a photograph of Mahler, a picture M. had made with colored chalk. Some birds' nests hung in the corners. I lit the lamp. I was done.

There is something you can tell people over and over, and with feeling and eloquence, and still never say it well enough for it to be more than news from abroad—people have no readiness for it, no empathy. It is the news of personal aging—of climbing, and knowing it, to some unrepeatable pitch and coming forth on the other side, which is pleasant still but which is, unarguably, different—which is the beginning of descent. It is the news that no one is singular, that no argument will change the course, that one's time is more gone than not, and what is left waits to be spent gracefully and attentively, if not quite so actively. The plumbers in town now are the sons of our old plumber. I cut some pine boards for some part of an hour, and I am tired. A year or so ago, hammering, I hit my thumb, directly and with force, and lost the nail for a half year. I was recently given a power drill, which also sets and removes screws. It could be a small cannon, so apprehensive am I of its fierce and quick power. When I handle it well (which to begin with means that I aim it correctly), difficult tasks are made easy. But when I do not, I hold an angry weasel in my hand.

I hardly used the little house—it became a place to store garden tools, boxes of this or that. Did I write one poem there? Yes, I did, and a few more. But its purpose never was to be shelter for thought. I built it *to build it,* stepped out over the threshold, and was gone.

I don't think I am old yet, or done with growing. But my perspective has altered—I am less hungry for the busyness of the body, more interested in the tricks of the mind. I am gaining, also, a new affection for wood that is useless, that has been tossed out, that merely exists, quietly, wherever it has ended up. Planks on the beach rippled and salt-soaked. Pieces of piling, full of the tunnels of shipworm. In the woods, fallen branches of oak, of maple, of the dear, wind-worn pines. They lie on the ground and do nothing. They are travelers on the way to oblivion.

The young man now—that carpenter we began with—places his notebook carefully beside him and rises and, as though he had just come back from some great distance, looks around. There are his tools, there is the wood; there is his unfinished task, to which, once more, he turns his attention. But life is no narrow business. On any afternoon he may hear and follow this same rhapsody, turning from his usual labor, swimming away into the pleasures, the current of language. More power to him!

For myself, I have passed him by and have gone into the woods. Near the path, one of the tall maples has fallen. It is early spring, so the crimped, maroon flowers are just emerging. Here and there slabs of the bark have exploded away in the impact of its landing. But, mostly, it lies as it stood, though not such a net for the wind as it was. What is it now? What does it signify? Not Indolence, surely, but something, all the same, that balances with Ambition.

Call it Rest. I sit on one of the branches. My idleness suits me. I am content. I have built my house. The blue butterflies, called azures, twinkle up from the secret place where they have been waiting. In their small blue dresses they float among the branches, they come close to me, one rests for a moment on my wrist. They do not recognize me as anything very different from this enfoldment of leaves, this wind-roarer, this wooden palace lying down, now, upon the earth, like anything heavy, and happy, and full of sunlight, and half asleep.

Sister Turtle

I

FOR SOME YEARS NOW I have eaten almost no meat. Though, occasionally, I crave it. It is a continually interesting subject of deep ambiguity. The poet Shelley believed his body would at last be the total and docile servant of his intellect if he ate nothing but leaves and fruit—and I am devoted to Shelley. But I am devoted to Nature too, and to consider Nature without this appetite—this other-creature-consuming appetite—is to look with shut eyes upon the miraculous interchange that makes things work, that causes one thing to nurture another, that creates the future out of the past. Still, in my personal life, I am often stricken with a wish to be *beyond all that*. I am burdened with anxiety. Anxiety for the lamb with his bitter future, anxiety for my own body, and, not least, anxiety for my own soul. You can fool a lot of yourself but you can't fool the soul. That worrier.

At the edge of the land lie the watery palaces—the ocean shore, the salt marsh, the black-bellied pond. And in them and upon them: clams, mussels, fish of all shapes and sizes, snails, turtles, frogs, eels, crabs, lobsters, worms, all crawling and diving and squirming among the cattails, sea rocks, seaweeds, sea pickles, *spartina,* lamb's-quarters, sour grass, arrowhead, mallow. Something eats each of these, each of these eats something else. This is our world. The orange mussel has a blue-black fringe along its body, and a heart and a lung, and a stomach. The scallop as it snaps its way through the water, when the east wind blows, gazes around with its dozens of pale blue eyes. The clam, sensing the presence of your hands, or the approach of the iron tine, presses deeper into the sand. Just where does self-awareness begin and end? With the June bug? With the shining, task-ridden ant? With the little cloud of gnats that drifts over the pond? I am one of those who has no trouble imagining the sentient lives of trees, of their leaves in some fashion communicating or of the massy trunks and heavy branches knowing it is I who have come, as I always come, each morning, to walk beneath them, glad to be alive and glad to be there.

All this, as prelude to the turtles.

2

They come, lumbering, from the many ponds. They dare the dangers of path, dogs, the highway, the accumulating heat that their bodies cannot regulate, or the equally stunning, always possible, cold.

Take one, then. She has reached the edge of the road, now she slogs up the impossible hill. When she slides back she rests for a while then trundles forward again. Emerging wet from the glittering caves of the pond, she travels in a coat of glass and dust. Where the sand clings thickly the mosquitoes, that hover about her like a gray veil, are frustrated. Not about her eyes, though, for as she blinks the sand falls; so at her tough, old face-skin those winged needles hang until their bodies fill, like tiny vials, with her bright blood. Each of the turtles is a female, and gravid, and is looking for a place to dig her nest; each of the mosquitoes is a female also who cannot, without one blood meal, lay her own fertile eggs upon the surface of some quiet pond.

Once, in spring, I saw the rhapsodic prelude to this enterprise of nest-building: two huge snapping turtles coupling. As they floated on the surface of the pond their occasional motions set them tumbling and heaving over and around again and yet again. The male's front feet gripped the rim of the female's shell as he pressed his massive body tightly against hers. For most of the afternoon they floated so, like a floundered craft—splashing and drifting through the murky water, or hanging motionless among the rising carpets of the pond lilies.

On these first hot days of summer, anywhere along the edges of these ponds or on the slopes of the dunes, I come upon the traveling turtles. I am glad to see them and sorry at the same time—my presence may be a disturbance that sends them back to the ponds before the egg laying has been accomplished, and what help is this to the world? Sometimes they will make the attempt again, sometimes they will not. If not, the eggs will dissolve back into other substances, inside their bodies.

There are other interrupters, far craftier than I. Whether the turtles come through sunlight or, as is more likely, under the moon's cool but sufficient light, raccoons follow. The turtles are scarcely done, scarcely gone, before the raccoons set their noses to the ground, and sniff, and discover, and dig, and devour, with rapacious and happy satisfaction.

And still, every year, there are turtles enough in the ponds.

As there are raccoons enough, sleeping the afternoons away high in the leafy trees.

One April morning I came upon a snapping turtle shell at the shore of Pasture Pond, tugged from the water, I imagine, by these same raccoons. Front to back, it measured more than thirty inches. Later I found leg bones nearby, also claws, and scutes, as they are called—the individual shingles that cover the raw bone of the shell. Perhaps the old giant died during a hard winter, frozen first at the edges and then thoroughly, in some too shallow cove. Or perhaps it died simply in the amplitude of time itself—turtles, like other reptiles, never stop growing, which makes for interesting imagined phenomena, if one's inclination is to the bizarre. But the usual is news enough. The adult snapping turtle can weigh ninety pounds, is omnivorous, and may live for decades. Or, to put it another way, who knows? The shell I found that April morning was larger than any of my field guides indicates is likely, or even possible.

3

I saw the tracks immediately—they swirled back and forth across the shuffled sand of the path. They seemed the design of indecision, but I am not sure. In three places a little digging had taken place. A false nest? A foot giving a swipe or two of practice motion? A false visual clue for the predator to come?

I leashed my two dogs and looked searchingly until I saw her, at one side of the path, motionless and sand-spattered. Already she was in the nest—or, more likely, leaving it. For she will dig through the sand until she all but vanishes—sometimes until there is nothing visible but the top of her head. Then, when the nesting is done, she thrusts the front part of her body upward so that she is positioned almost vertically, like a big pie pan on edge. Beneath her, as she heaves upward, the sand falls into the cavity of the nest, upon the heaped, round eggs.

She sees me, and does not move. The eyes, though they throw small light, are deeply alive and watchful. If she had to die in this hour and for this enterprise, she would, without hesitation. She would slide from life into death, still with that pin of light in each uncordial eye, intense and as loyal to the pumping of breath as anything in this world.

When our eyes meet, what can pass between us? She sees me as a danger, and she is right. If I come any closer, she will dismiss me peacefully if she can by retracting into her shell. But this is difficult; her bulky body will not fit entirely inside the recesses of that bony hut. She retreats, but still her head is outside, and a portion of each leg. She might hiss, or she might not. She might open the mighty beak of her mouth to give warning, and I might stare a moment into the clean, pale, glossy tunnel of her inner mouth, with its tag of tongue, before that head, that unexpected long neck flashes out—flashes, I say —and strikes me, hand or foot. She is snake-swift and accurate, and can bite cleanly through a stick three inches thick. Many a dog walks lame from such an encounter. I keep my dogs leashed and walk on. We turn the corner and vanish under the trees. It is five A.M.; for me, the beginning of the day — for her, the end of the long night.

Of appetite — of my own appetite — I recognize this: it flashes up, quicker than thought; it cannot be exiled; it can be held on leash, but only barely. Once, on an October day, as I was crossing a field, a red-tailed hawk rattled up from the ground. In the grass lay a pheasant, its breast already opened, only a little of the red, felt-like meat stripped away. It simply flew into my mind — that the pheasant, thus discovered, was to be *my* dinner! I swear, I felt the sweet prick of luck! Only secondly did I interrupt myself, and glance at the hawk, and walk on. Good for me! But I know how sparkling was the push of my own appetite. I am no fool, no sentimentalist. I know that appetite is one of the gods, with a rough and savage face, but a god all the same.

Teilhard de Chardin says somewhere that man's most agonizing spiritual dilemma is his necessity for food, with its unavoidable attachments to suffering. Who would disagree.

A few years ago I heard a lecture about the Whitney family, especially about Gloria Vanderbilt Whitney, whose patronage established the museum of that name in New York City. The talk was given by Mrs. Whitney's granddaughter, and she used a fine phrase when speaking of her family — of their sense of "inherited responsibility" — to do, of course, with received wealth and a sense of using it for public good. Ah! Quickly I slipped this phrase from the air and put it into my own pocket!

For it is precisely how I feel, who have inherited not measurable wealth but, as we all do who care for it, that immeasurable fund of thoughts and ideas, from writers and thinkers long gone into the ground—and, inseparable from those wisdoms because *demanded* by them, the responsibility to live thoughtfully and intelligently. To enjoy, to question—never to assume, or trample. Thus the great ones (*my* great ones, who may not be the same as *your* great ones) have taught me—to observe with passion, to think with patience, to live always care-ingly.

So here I am, walking on down the sandy path, with my wild body, with the inherited devotions of curiosity and respect. The moment is full of such exquisite interest as Fabre or Flaubert would have been utterly alive to. Yes, it is a din of voices that I hear, and they do not all say the same thing. But the fit of thoughtfulness unites them.

Who are they? For me they are Shelley, and Fabre, and Wordsworth—the young Wordsworth—and Barbara Ward, and Blake, and Basho, Maeterlinck and Jastrow, and sweetest Emerson, and Carson, and Aldo Leopold. Forebears, models, spirits whose influence and teachings I am now inseparable from, and forever grateful for. I go nowhere, I arrive nowhere, without them. With them I live my life, with them I enter the event, I mold the meditation, I keep if I can some essence of the hour, even as it slips away. And I do not accomplish this alert and loving confrontation by myself and alone, but through terrifying and continual effort, and with this innumerable, fortifying company, bright as stars in the heaven of my mind.

Were they seed eaters? Were they meat eaters? Not the point. They were dreamers, and imaginers, and declarers; they lived looking and looking and looking, seeing the apparent and beyond the apparent, wondering, allowing for uncertainty, also grace, easygoing here, ferociously unmovable there; they were thoughtful. A few voices, strict and punctilious, like Shelley's, like Thoreau's, cry out: *Change! Change!* But most don't say that; they simply say: Be what you are, of the earth, but a dreamer too. Teilhard de Chardin was not talking about how to escape anguish, but about how to live with it.

4

I went back, toward evening, and dug in the sand to the depth of nine inches more or less, and found nothing. There, a few unbroken roots told me the turtle's paddle-shaped feet had gone no farther down. There, as I imagine it, she had shifted the angle of her digging. Perhaps she rested first. Then she began again her sweep-shoving, digging a smaller chamber opening from the original, but narrower, a *sanctum,* to the front of the first. When she was done, a short fleshy tube descended from her body and reached to this chamber, where the expelled eggs piled up rapidly on the nest of sand.

Into this passage I dug, until my fingers felt the first of the eggs — round, slightly soft — then I began to feel more, and I began to remove them. There were twenty-seven, smaller than ping-pong balls, which they somewhat resembled. They were not altogether opaque, but cast a slightly yellow interior light. I placed thirteen in my pocket, carefully, and replaced fourteen in the nest, repacked the nest with sand, and swept from the surface all sign of my digging.

I scrambled them. They were a meal. Not too wonderful, not too bad. Rich, substantial. I could not crack the shells, but had to make a knife slit to enter into each bright chamber. The yolks were large, the whites of the egg scant; the little fertility knot, the bud of the new turtle, was no more apparent than it is in a fertile chicken's egg. There was, in the fabric of the eggs scrambled, a sense of fiber, a tactility, as though a sprinkle of cornmeal had been tossed in, and had not quite dissolved. I imagined it as the building material of the shell. The eggs were small enough that thirteen made no greedy portion. I ate them all, with attention, whimsy, devotion, and respect.

The next morning I went back to the path. I wanted to see how the nest-place was after one sheet of darkness had gone over it. None of the other prowlers—raccoons, that is—had discovered it. By end of summer, under the provisions of good fortune, the hatchlings, fourteen of them, would rise through the sand. Hardly pausing to consider the world that so suddenly appeared around them, they would turn unerringly toward the dark and rich theater of the nearest pond, would hasten to its edge, and dive in.

Now, in the last hot days of June, I see no more turtles on the paths, nor even their curvaceous wandering trails over the dunes. Now the heat brings forth other buddings and advancements. Almost overnight the honey locust trees have let down their many tassels of blossoms, small white flasks filled with the sweetest honey. I gather handfuls and, for a second, hold them against my face. The fringes of paradise: summer on earth. They, too, will nourish me. Last week I ate the eggs of the turtle, like little golden suns; today, the honey locust blossoms, in batter, will make the finest crepes of the most common pancakes. My body, which must be fed, will be well fed. The hawk, in the pale pink evening, went back to the body of the pheasant. The turtle lay a long time on the bottom of the pond, resting. Then she turned, her eyes upon some flickering nearby as, without terror, without sorrow, but in the voracious arms of the first of the earth's gods, she did what she must, she did what all must do. All things are meltable, and replaceable. Not at this moment, but soon enough, we are lambs and we are leaves, and we are stars, and the shining, mysterious pond water itself.

The Swan

Y EARS AGO I set three "rules" for myself. Every poem I write, I said, must have a genuine body, it must have sincere energy, and it must have a spiritual purpose. If a poem to my mind failed any one of these categories it was rebuked and re-done, or discarded. Over the forty or so years during which writing poems has been my primary activity, I have added other admonitions and consents. I want every poem to "rest" in intensity. I want it to be rich with "pictures of the world." I want it to carry threads from the perceptually felt world to the intellectual world. I want each poem to indicate a life lived with intelligence, patience, passion, and whimsy (not my life—not necessarily!—but the life of my *formal self,* the writer).

I want the poem to ask something and, at its best moments, I want the question to remain unanswered. I want it to be clear that answering the question is the reader's part in an implicit author-reader pact. Last but not least, I want the poem to have a pulse, a breathiness, some moment of earthly delight. (While one is luring the reader into the enclosure of serious subjects, pleasure is by no means an unimportant ingredient.)

"The Swan" has some of these qualities. It has as well a "secret" humor; I was watching geese not swans when I began the poem—that is, thought of the poem, felt it in concept, and wrote down a few lines. Since I had only recently written a poem about geese, I thought I would intensify the poem's display, and make something even fancier than wild geese out of the beautiful bird shapes I was watching. I thought this fairly funny, and I remember it was therefore with a certain light-hearted pleasure that I proceeded with the description. Though unknown as a fact to the reader, I don't wonder at all if my mood attuned me more finely than otherwise to my work—I am sure it did.

The form was no problem—long sentences on short lines, a little enjambment to keep things going (the swan is in motion) but not too much, so that the lines, like the swan's movements, are decisive, and keep their dignity. Take out some commas, for smoothness and because almost every poem in the universe moves too slowly. Then, once the "actual" is in place (in words), begin to address the reason for taking the reader's good and valuable time—invite the reader to want to do something beyond merely receiving beauty, and to configure in his or her own mind what that might be. Make sure there is nothing in the poem that would keep the reader from becoming the speaker of the poem. And, that's all. The final phrase—"touch the shore"—is vital; it is a closure yet it is also a moment of arrival, and therefore a possible new beginning.

The poem in which the reader does not feel himself or herself a participant is a lecture, listened to from an uncomfortable chair, in a stuffy room, inside a building. My poems have all been written—if not finished at least started—somewhere out-of-doors: in the fields, on the shore, under the sky. They are not lectures. The point is not what the poet would make of the moment but what the reader would make of it. If the reader accepts and thinks about its question, "The Swan" accomplishes what it set out to do.

The Swan

Across the wide waters
  something comes
    floating—a slim
    and delicate

ship, filled
  with white flowers—
    and it moves
      on its miraculous muscles

as though time didn't exist,
  as though bringing such gifts
    to the dry shore
      was a happiness

almost beyond bearing.
  And now it turns its dark eyes,
    it rearranges
      the clouds of its wings,

it trails
  an elaborate webbed foot,
    the color of charcoal.
      Soon it will be here.

Oh, what shall I do
  when that poppy-colored beak
    rests in my hand?
      Said Mrs. Blake of the poet:

I miss my husband's company—
  he is so often
    in paradise.
      Of course! the path to heaven

doesn't lie down in flat miles.
    It's in the imagination
        with which you perceive
            this world,

and the gestures
    with which you honor it.
        Oh, what will I do, what will I say, when those
            white wings
        touch the shore?

Three Prose Poems

I

Oh, yesterday, that one, we all cry out. *Oh, that one!* How rich and possible everything was! How ripe, ready, lavish, and filled with excitement—how hopeful we were on those summer days, under the clean, white racing clouds. *Oh, yesterday!*

2

I was in the old burn-dump—no longer used—where the honeysuckle all summer is in a moist rage, willing it would seem to be enough to decorate the whole world. Here a pair of hummingbirds lived every summer, as if the only ones of their kind, in their own paradise at the side of the high road. On hot afternoons, beside the blackberry canes that rose thickly from that wrecked place, I strolled, and was almost always sure to see the male hummingbird on his favorite high perch, near the top of a wild cherry tree, looking out across his kingdom with bright eye and even brighter throat. And then, on the afternoon I am telling about, as he swung his head, there came out of the heavens an immense growl, of metal and energy, shoving and shrilling, boring through the air. And a plane, a black triangle, flew screaming from the horizon, heavy talons clenched and lumpy on its underside. Immediately: a suffering in the head, through the narrow-channeled ears. And I saw the small bird, in the sparkle of its tree, fling its green head sideways for the eye to see this hawk-bird, this nightmare pressing overhead. And, lo, the hummingbird cringed, it

---

hugged itself to the limb, it hunkered, it quivered. It was God's gorgeous, flashing jewel: afraid.

All narrative is metaphor.

3

After the storm the ocean returned without fanfare to its old offices; the tide climbed onto the snow-covered shore and then receded; so there was the world: sky, water, the pale sand and, where the tide had reached that day's destination, the snow.

And this detail: the body of a duck, a golden-eye; and beside it one black-backed gull. In the body of the duck, among the breast feathers, a hole perhaps an inch across; the color within the hole a shouting red. And bend it as you might, nothing was to blame: storms must toss, and the great black-backed gawker must eat, and so on. It was merely a moment. The sun, angling out from the bunched clouds, cast one could easily imagine tenderly over the landscape its extraordinary light.

Moss

Maybe the idea of the world as flat isn't a tribal memory or an archetypal memory, but something far older—a fox memory, a worm memory, a moss memory.

Memory of leaping or crawling or shrugging rootlet by rootlet forward, across the flatness of everything.

To perceive of the earth as round needed something else —standing up!—that hadn't yet happened.

What a wild family! Fox and giraffe and wart hog, of course. But these also: bodies like tiny strings, bodies like blades and blossoms! Cord grass, Christmas fern, soldier moss! And here comes grasshopper, all toes and knees and eyes, over the little mountains of the dust.

When I see the black cricket in the woodpile, in autumn, I don't frighten her. And when I see the moss grazing upon the rock, I touch her tenderly,

sweet cousin.

Once

What is autobiography anyway but a story rich and impossible of completion—an intense, careful, expressive, self-interested failure? What can I say to you, therefore, that will be true, and will cast its shadow or its light over the whole body of my telling, of my being here, of who I am?

> When the young deer hung herself on the fence, catching one foreleg in a loop of wire, and the rough farm dogs were running toward her, I knew the only things I could do: hide my eyes, or run. And I ran, faster than ever before in my life, and flung my body against hers, so that we were both pressed against the mesh of the fence while the dogs raced back and forth. But the deer did not know my meaning, or if she did she still could not tolerate my nearness; she hooted like a goat, and yanked her foot free, and dashed away into the woods.

> A few days later, I saw her in a field. In spite of the beads of blood that were left on the fence where she had pulled her snagged foot free, she was fine, she was nimble and quick; she was beautiful.

> And I thought: I shall remember this all my life. The peril, the running, the howling of the dogs, the smothering. Then the happiness—of action, of leaping. Then the green sweetness of distance. And the trees: their thickness and their compassion, all around.

The Whistler

All of a sudden she began to whistle. By all of a sudden I mean that for more than thirty years she had not whistled. It was thrilling. At first I wondered, who was in the house, what stranger? I was upstairs reading, and she was downstairs. As from the throat of a wild and cheerful bird, not caught but visiting, the sound warbled and slid and doubled back and larked and soared.

Finally I said, Is that you? Is that you whistling? Yes, she said. I used to whistle, a long time ago. Now I see I can still whistle. And cadence after cadence she strolled through the house, whistling.

I know her so well, I think. I thought. Elbow and ankle. Mood and desire. Anguish and frolic. Anger too. And the devotions. And for all that, do we even begin to know each other? Who is this I've been living with for thirty years?

This clear, dark, lovely whistler?

PART TWO

Four Poets

The Bright Eyes of Eleonora:
Poe's Dream of Recapturing the Impossible

I

IN POE'S STORIES and poems we hear continually about compulsion, terrors loosed by the powerful upon the weak (or the powerful components of the mind upon the weak components of the mind); we hear about plague, and tortures, and revenge. But none of these elements does more than forward the real subject of Poe's work, which is the anguish of knowing nothing for sure about the construct of the universe, or about the existence of a moral order within it—anything that would clarify its seemingly total and imperial indifference toward individual destiny.

Poe is no different from any of us—we all choke in such vapors, somewhat, sometimes. A normal life includes the occasional black mood. But most of us have had some real enough experience with certainty, which helps us to sustain ourselves through passages of metaphysical gloom. While Poe had none. Not little, but none.

This lack disordered him. It is not a spiritual lack, but rather a lack of emotional organization, of confidence. And not self-confidence, which is already a complicated asset, but a lack of confidence in the world entire, and its benevolent as well as malevolent possibilities. In the deepest sense, Poe was without confidence in a future that might be different from the past. He was, forever, reliving an inescapable, original woe.

At the same time he was both a powerful constructor of narrative and a perfect acrobat of language. He was also a man of enormous courage. With almost superhuman will he wrote his poems and his stories—I almost want to say *he wrote and rewrote his story and his poem*—trying to solve the unsolvable and move on. But he never moved on. He never solved anything.

2

His mother, Eliza Poe, an actress, died when Edgar was two years old. She was twenty-four. It was a pitiful finish to a miserable story: Eliza Poe was penniless, consumptive, and abandoned by Edgar's father, whose occasional and itinerant occupation was also acting.

In Richmond, Virginia, where Eliza died, Poe was taken to live with the John Allan family, perhaps by the whim of Frances Allan, who had no children and had witnessed the death of Eliza. The relationship between Poe and John Allan, a successful merchant, was perpetually and mutually difficult. Though he took the family's name, Poe was never legally adopted.

Poe became friends with a woman named Jane Stanard, the mother of a schoolboy friend. She was a strange, closeted, not too steady figure. Even as their friendship deepened, Jane Stanard sickened, was declared insane, and died. Frances Allan also had never been robust. When Poe was twenty years old, and away from home, Frances Allan died. It was a separation without closure, since John Allan chose not to summon Poe home in time for a last meeting before the final and implacable silence of death.

In 1834, when he was twenty-five, Poe married his cousin Virginia Clemm; she was thirteen years old. Does the future seem ensured? Eight years later, while Virginia was singing, blood began to run from her mouth. It was, it is fair to say, consumption. In 1847 Virginia died. She was twenty-five.

Poe had two years to live. With terrifying gusto, he drank his way through them.

In the Free Library of Philadelphia there is a portrait of the actress Eliza Poe. She is at once curiously stiff and visibly animated; her long black hair curls at the ends and frames the wide brow and the enormous dark eyes. The same dark curls, the same large eyes — in fact, a very similar white, low-bodiced dress — appear in another painting, this one in Richmond, of Frances Allan. And Virginia Clemm? She is described as having had a chalky white complexion, and long black hair, and a high, clear brow, and large eyes that grew even larger and ever more luminous during her illness.

To readers of Poe's poems and tales, it is an altogether familiar face:

The forehead was high, and very pale, and singularly placid; and the once jetty hair fell partially over it, and overshadowed the hollow temples with innumerable ringlets, now of a vivid yellow, and jarring discordantly, in their fantastic character, with the melancholy of the countenance. ("Berenice")*

I examined the contour of the lofty and pale forehead — it was faultless — how cold indeed that word when applied to a majesty so divine! — the skin rivalling the purest ivory, the commanding extent and repose, the gentle prominence of the regions above the temples; and the raven-black, the glossy, the luxuriant, and naturally-curling tresses, setting forth the full force of the Homeric epithet, "hyacinthine"! ("Ligeia")

If the faces of Poe's women are often strikingly similar, other characteristics are no less consistent:

> Lo! in yon brilliant window-niche
> How *statue-like* I see thee stand!   ("To Helen")†

So Poe writes of that pale beauty — that Helen, who is also Lenore in "The Raven" and Eleonora in the story named for her. And the Lady Madeline in "The Fall of the House of Usher" comes from the grave "a *lofty* and enshrouded figure." And Ligeia "came and departed as a shadow." And her eyes were large — "far larger than the ordinary eyes of our own race." There is not the briefest glimpse of Annabel Lee in the rhapsodic, death-soaked poem of that name, yet we know, don't we, what she must have looked like. Pale, dark-haired, with wide and luminous eyes — vivacious in the trembling, fragile way of mayflies. The narrator says of Berenice: "Oh, gorgeous yet fan-

---

*All quotations are taken from *The Collected Tales and Poems of Edgar Allan Poe* (New York: Modern Library, 1992).

†All italics in quotations are mine.

tastic beauty! oh, sylph amid the shrubberies of Arnheim! Oh, Naiad among its fountains!" Of Eleonora: "like the ephemeron, she had been made perfect in loveliness only to die." Of Ligeia again: she has "the face of the water-nymph, that lives but an hour" and "the beauty of the fabulous Houri of the Turk."

In Poe's stories overall, no focus is so constant as that of the face and, within the face, the look of the eyes. "The *expression* in the eyes of Ligeia!" the narrator cries aloud and, sacrificing the "blue-eyed Lady Rowena," wills the dead, dark-eyed Ligeia to return to him within the vehicle of Rowena's body. When the corpse stirs slowly and opens its eyes, he shrieks—of course it is the end of the story—"these are the full, and the black, and the wild eyes of my lost love."

Nothing, nothing in all the secret and beautiful and peaceful Valley of the Many-Colored Grass, where the narrator is but a boy and loves for the first time—nothing shines so brightly as the eyes of the first-beloved, Eleonora.

3

Said the poet Robert Frost, "We begin in infancy by establishing correspondence of eyes with eyes."* It is deeply true. It is where the confidence comes from; the child whose gaze is met learns that the world is real, and desirable—that the child himself is real, and cherished. The look in the eyes of Poe's heroines —it is the same intensity, over and over, upon the long string

---

Robert Frost: Collected Poems, Prose, & Plays (New York: Library of America, 1995), p. 742.

of his many tales. It is the look that, briefly, begins to give such confidence — then fades.

Not in "Ligeia" and "Berenice" and "Eleonora" only, but in other stories too, the eye is a critical feature. In "The Tell-Tale Heart," the narrator murders an old man of whom he is truly fond because of the blue veil that is a cast over one eye. "The vulture eye," he calls it.

> Whenever it fell upon me, my blood ran cold; and so by degrees — very gradually — I made up my mind to take the life of the old man, and thus rid myself of the eye for ever.

It is a simple case. The eye that does not look back does not acknowledge. To Poe's narrator, it is unbearable.

The eyes of Augustus Bedloe, in "A Tale of the Ragged Mountains," are

> abnormally large, and round like those of a cat.... In moments of excitement the orbs grew bright to a degree almost inconceivable; seeming to emit luminous rays, not of a reflected but of an intrinsic lustre, as does a candle or the sun.

Bedloe, otherwise a corpse-like figure, gains vigor through his daily use of morphine. He is, we understand, a man who is being medically supervised; he has even been hypnotized. He tells his story: one afternoon, in the mountains of Virginia, he breaks through the wall of time and place. "You will say now, of course, that I dreamed; but not so," he says. But his inexorable original fate, in the trivia of this new time and place, the Virginia wilderness, waits for him. He cannot escape it.

In "The Fall of the House of Usher," the gloomy mansion itself takes on the look of a face, with its "vacant and eye-like windows." The same face makes its grim appearance in the poem "The Haunted Palace." In the tale "William Wilson," on the other hand, such play of eye correspondence is significantly lacking; the two William Wilsons of the story are, of course, one person.

Neither does the flash of the eye, luminous or overcast, play a role in "The Pit and the Pendulum."

> At length, with a wild desperation at heart, I quickly un-
> closed my eyes. My worst thoughts, then, were confirmed.
> The blackness of eternal night encompassed me.

Underneath its ropes and rats, its tensions and extraordinary machineries, "The Pit and the Pendulum" is the story of the soul struggling with the tortures of an indifferent universe. It is a tale of unmatchable horror — as it is equally a tale of all but unmatchable endurance. In the context of Poe's work as a whole, both the "eternal night" and the narrator's solitude are elements that make of the pit's chamber an even more terrible tableau. In the blackness of the pit there is nothing — and no one. Not even the eye with the blue veil.

4

It is not hard to recognize Poe's many narrators as a single sensibility, as one character, and to see this character as other than rational. He is a man of nervous temperament; he is capable of great love, loyalty, grief, of "wild excitement" (a recurring phrase); he owns a strange and unfettered imagination. His enterprise is to challenge and dissolve a particular fact or circumstance that represents the natural order of things—specifically, death's irreversibility. He therefore seeks to understand the world in a way that will disprove such circumstance. Discovering a "different" world assumes *experiencing manifestations of that different world*. To begin, then, it is necessary to disassociate from the world as it is ordinarily experienced. And, not casually. He must unstring the universe to its farthest planet and star, and restring it in another way.

His posture is transcendentalism, of the nineteenth-century Germanic variety. The possibilities of alchemy, mesmerism, occultism, appeal to him. He is no Orpheus, begging an exception and a second chance, but rather—I mean from his own view—a visionary. To change his own fate, he would change our comprehension of the entire world.

The question of madness is always present. The actions of the narrator are often recognizably insane. But the definitions of madness and rationality have been thrown here into the wind; in Poe's stories, such states are uncertainly bordered areas in which, suddenly, ghosts walk. "Men have called me mad; but the question is not yet settled, whether madness is or is not the loftiest intelligence," the narrator says in "Eleonora."

Illness, as well, is a presence, an excuse for clearly inexcusable actions. The narrator in "Berenice" is named Agaeus, a word wondrously close to "aegis," which, in English schools, is a term meaning a note that signifies sickness as an excuse. It is an uncommon term, but Poe, who went to school in England for five years while the Allans were living in London, no doubt knew it.

Upon the wing of such pure or near madness, the effort toward re-visioning goes on. The mind deranged, by alcohol, opium or morphine, or insanity, sees a world differently from the sane and the sober—*but, in fact, it does see a world.* Poe's narrators drink furiously and, when they can get it, they take into their bodies the white powder opium; thus they lean, trembling, against the walls of ordinary perception. And thus, over and over, with "wild excitement," they "swoon" out of this world.

To swoon is not only to pass from consciousness physically; it may also represent a willingness, even an eagerness, to experience unknown parts of life—obscure regions that might lead one toward a re-visioning. One swoons for many reasons and from many causes—from fever, sheer fright, extreme agitation, from exertion or exhaustion. The effects of opium and alcohol alone, in sufficient doses, will also bring on a kind of swooning; one leaves the realm of the rational and the known for that shapeless, unmapped region of "seeming." What is certain in the rational realm is by no means certain in the kingdom of swoon. *And though nothing in that dark kingdom is provable, neither can its nonexistence be proven.* If nothing there is solid to the hand, it is solid enough to the mind, and upon that smallest beginning the need of the mind builds.

Poe's fascination with enclosed space (the brain shape) as pit, maelstrom, catacomb, ballroom (in "Hop-Frog"), and the many chambers and turrets of castles, reaches a curious pitch in a piece called "Philosophy of Furniture." Here Poe describes, in intense and elaborate detail, his "favorite room." The description is obsessional. Here are carpets and curtains in mute and lustrous colors, paintings, furniture, giltwork and fringe, draperies, mirrors, Sèvres vases, candelabra; we are given not only their exact shapes and colors but their precise placement within the room. It is a room where "repose speaks in all." Yet it is not a bedroom—there is no bed here for sleeping on in the ordinary way of well-earned and deep rest. There are two sofas and, upon one, says Poe, the proprietor lies asleep. But it is sleep as Poe most sought and valued it—not for the sake of rest, but for escape. Sleep, too, is a kind of swooning out of this world.

5

Poe's work is exquisitely and opulently constructed; the narratives have a fascination that is a sure-hold—a quality that, for lack of another word, one might simply call entertainment. They are frightening—but not in the way that Kafka's "The Metamorphosis," for example, or James's "The Turn of the Screw" is frightening. In spite of the extreme and macabre symbolism in Kafka's story, both "The Metamorphosis" and "The Turn of the Screw" take place in a world uncomfortably familiar, and the stories unfold, both of them, in a terrifyingly low-key, unextraordinary way. They are, horribly and unmistakably, descriptions of life as we know it, or *could* easily know it. While Poe's stories are—stories. Full of the hardware of the nightmare —graves, corpses, storms, moldering castles, catacombs—and hovering always at the edge of tension and incredulity, they never fail to thrill as *stories*.

But literature, the best of it, does not aim to be literature. It wants and strives, beyond that artifact part of itself, to be a true part of the composite human record—that is, not words but a reality.

Poe's work opens on this deeper level when we consider what we know about his life. Such consideration is a tricky business. In our own age such investigation and correspondence is, I think, grossly overdone; hardly a literary melancholy these days is explained in any terms but those of personal grievance. But Poe's case is exceptional. Life-grief was his earliest and his deepest life experience. Not to wonder how deeply it shaped his outlook and his work is to miss something sharply sorrowful, and deeply valiant.

But let us consider the matter in yet another way. Poe's inability to incorporate loss and move on was not a response born of his experience alone, but was also an invention, an endlessly repeatable dark adventure created by his exceedingly fertile mind. For Poe, in an artistically kaleidoscopic brilliance, does not write only about his own argument with the universe, but about everyone's argument.

For are we not all, at times, exactly like Poe's narrators—beating upon the confining walls of circumstance, the limits of the universe? In spiritual work, with good luck (or grace), we come to accept life's brevity for ourselves. But the lover that is in each of us—the part of us that *adores* another person—ah! that is another matter.

In the mystery and the energy of loving, we all view time's shadow upon the beloved as wretchedly as any of Poe's narrators. We do not think of it every day, but we never forget it: the beloved shall grow old, or ill, and be taken away finally. No matter how ferociously we fight, how tenderly we love, how bitterly we argue, how pervasively we berate the universe, how cunningly we hide, this is what shall happen. In the wide circles of timelessness, everything material and temporal will fail, including the manifestation of the beloved. In this universe we are given two gifts: the ability to love, and the ability to ask questions. Which are, at the same time, the fires that warm us and the fires that scorch us. This is Poe's real story. As it is ours. And this is why we honor him, why we are fascinated far past the simple narratives. He writes about our own inescapable destiny.

His words and his valor are all he has, and they are stunning. When in "The Masque of the Red Death" the stranger who is really nothing but an empty cloak enters and slays the Prince, it is Poe and it is ourselves with him who rush forward and batter hopelessly against that incomprehensibility, with our frail fists, with "the wild courage of despair."

A Man Named Frost

IN THE LYRICAL POEMS of Robert Frost there is almost always something wrong, a dissatisfaction or distress. The poet attempts an explanation and a correction. He is not successful. But he has, often in metaphoric language, named whatever it is that disquiets him. At the same time, in the same passages, the poem is so pleasant—so very pleasant—to read or to hear.

In fact we are hearing two different messages: *everything is all right,* say the meter and the rhyme; *everything is not all right,* say the words. This makes of the poem a complex discourse, although it is not felt to be so by the general public, who hear and feel more emphatically than they comprehend. Frost, it is believed by the thousands who love his work, is easily understandable; he is clear, musical, and bittersweet; in poem after poem he is felt to be rejoicing, if in a rather sad way, over the affairs of the world, especially the natural world.

I do not find that he rejoices at all. What feels like rejoicing is the manner in which Frost describes the indifference and, just as attentively, the prettiness of the world. He does this through exact and often emblematic description, and by his habit of pausing—in fields, on hillsides, by woods. There is everywhere in Frost a sense that a man has time to look at things, to think and to feel. This, indeed, is the important Frostian work. But still, for all the world is full of handsome (or winsome, or profound) places, the speaker—this speaker, anyway—cannot unstick himself from his discomfort.

And the distress is never of the moment, but lifelong. It is philosophical and unsolvable. "Life," the poems seem to say, "is a descent. It is full of intimate and memorable details, but they are mutable, all of them, and woe is only followed in its course by more, and worse." This is the message I get from Frost, in poem after poem.

But: that reliable and easily accessible tone of the poet's voice! That steady iambic! Those rhymes, comforting as handshakes! That diction so familiar to us all! Frost is eminently recognizable. The meditations, contemplations, devotions, revelations, outcries and love laments are uttered plainly, always in Frost's unmistakable clear, heavy-hearted voice. And we do like that. We like that very much. We like the poet to be avuncular and familiar as well as magical. To recognize the voice is halfway to understanding what is being said. So we think.

For decades Frost was this country's most beloved and popular poet. He enjoyed this popularity, and it enhanced him. After the long succession of years without publication, without any sort of literary reputation, he could never get enough of it: recognition, a response from the crowd. Though he never lost the capacity to speak in a voice that was tender and vulnerable —it is the voice we hear in "Bereft" and "My November Guest" and "Nothing Gold Can Stay" and "To Earthward"—he added greatly to his range: wit, polish, humor, malice, snobbery, an assumption of political savvy and philosophical acumen became part of him. All this late and heavy blossoming changed his voice; it changed the man too, no doubt. The later poems—beginning with the volume *West-Running Brook*, say—less commonly have that sense of a private man working at the conflicts of his life, which in the first books we are exquisitely privileged to overhear. The poems become, in the later books, entertainments and pronouncements. It is as though Frost felt himself obliged, as a public man, to display a reasonable cheerfulness, whatever he felt privately.

We know a great deal about Frost's life, yet without all the certainties that would allow our final guesses and surmises to be more than that. It is always so—biography must gather the facts as it can, then take the risk of summation. Thus Frost, whose public image for years was of a loving and lovable man, becomes the surly husband and father, the unforgiving, impatient, overtly ambitious man, if we believe what we read. Maybe it is true; probably it is partly true. But we would spend our time more profitably in the texts of his poems than in the chapters of his life. Surely every poem, from Smart's "Jubilate Agno" to Keats's "Ode to a Nightingale," is both experience and fabrication. We do not have the man, or at least we do not know for sure if or not we have him—we have his work. The voice of Frost's poems, whether or not it is Frost himself, is the voice of a man who finds life a trial, who finds the physical world handsome but fragile, who finds reality less than his expectation, who finds no easy solution to his desire for solitude and his longing for community, who finds love an agony, who finds no sweet that is not bonded to bitter.

Moreover, throughout Frost's work there is one element

missing altogether, and that is rapture. Not in the early poems, not in the late poems, in which there is sometimes a real abundance of play and pleasure, do we find it. No brimming satisfaction, no mad happiness, no bodied or unbodied joy. Wit there is, and wonder, and reason, and some brief moments of tranquility, and much hope, and endless bearing up under the weight of a life. But the great height is not there. The sharp spilling of the soul into the whistling air—the pure spine-involved and organ-attached bliss—is not there.

Instead its opposite—despair, wed to fortitude—is the dense emotion at the center of Frost's work and, as he displays it, equally at the center of the harsh rural New England landscapes of his books. The hill wife cannot bear her loneliness and runs into the ferny woods and is never seen again. The white spider, in a web strung upon the white weed called the heal-all, snags and feasts on the white moth. An acquaintance with the night walks the empty street with an ever-unanswered longing for some human connection. The poet is haunted by: the road not taken, the restlessness of the rooted trees, the quick descent of nature's gold, the peril of the runaway colt playing on the snowy hills, the desire for respite in the world of "easy wind and downy flake." In the dramatic poems, the hired man dies, the young boy whose hand is cut by the leaping buzz saw dies, the man whose feet were chopped in a factory accident settles for five hundred miserable dollars. And so on.

And all the while the language is as sweet as Herrick's, and the poems are deliciously *formed.* So often it seems Frost is about to float away upon a lilting cadence, or barge away in some desperate rage, and then he reins himself in; there is the wondrous restraint, the words that are rich and resonant: dar*k* and deep. And there is also that other restraint: the impending rhyme-match and the line length that must reach, but never overreach, its companions. Or if on a rare day lines are given small license, it will be by no more than a single stress; he will companion decasyllables with hendecasyllables, although this seems done more to sound out the elasticity of the vernacular than any letting down of the guard. As the left wall of his poems is strict, so is the right. In the issue of form, of what is built, declares the design of the Frost poem, we are sure, and secure. Whatever the painful and unresolved interior of the poem, the poet has kept his balance, and we can too. Balance, restraint, steadiness, a controlled and reasonable tongue, and an eye that never fails to see the beauty of things whatever else it sees — these are victories. Whatever disappointments and woe Frost felt, he rocked his way through them and made the perfect cages of his poems to hold them. He did not fall, and the poems do not fall. To all our great and fine poets we go for advisement, for some stay against the chaos of our own experience. This steadiness of design and sweetness of speech are Frost's gift to us.

But they are not the whole gift. Frost's prickly grief and his disconsolation must be added to them before we can understand the gift entire. A hundred times Frost's misery, absolutely his misery, catches up some merry sparkle. A hundred times he sinks, and yet again opens his eyes to the stars. Yes, one must embrace the darkness with the light to get all of Frost's gift. For it seems he could not hear the trill of the trees without the cry of the root, or see the golden leaves but with the sign of their death nearby, or witness easy wind and downy flake apart from the huge, cold, indifferent gears of nature spewing them out.

———

My November Guest

My Sorrow, when she's here with me,
    Thinks these dark days of autumn rain
Are beautiful as days can be;
She loves the bare, the withered tree;
    She walks the sodden pasture lane.

Her pleasure will not let me stay.
    She talks and I am fain to list:
She's glad the birds are gone away,
She's glad her simple worsted gray
    Is silver now with clinging mist.

The desolate, deserted trees,
    The faded earth, the heavy sky,
The beauties she so truly sees,
She thinks I have no eye for these,
    And vexes me for reason why.

Not yesterday I learned to know
    The love of bare November days
Before the coming of the snow,
But it were vain to tell her so,
    And they are better for her praise.

Robert Frost
From *A Boy's Will*

The Poem as Prayer, the Prayer as Ornament: Gerard Manley Hopkins

IN GERARD MANLEY HOPKINS'S world of Christian faith and Jesuit rigor there exists always the incomparable gift of Christ's love and sacrifice; it is the model for everything. And there is also ever present the story of Mary: her mercy and her power of intercession. Between these two presences Hopkins's poems praise and leap, praise and shiver, praise and kneel, praise and self-condemn. It is a poetry of rapture and pain, of the perfection of God and the awkwardnesses and imperfections of the poet.

When he joined the Jesuit order, Hopkins destroyed whatever poems he had previously written; he intended to write no more. Only Hopkins knew how large was the pressure in him to be a poet; only he knew whether it interfered with the wholeheartedness of his decision to become a Jesuit. So to wonder about his decision is unavailing. We do know this: when an opportunity came to write again—a remark by a bishop, in his presence, that he wished someone would keep alive the memory of the *Deutschland,* a storm-wrecked ship on which five Franciscan nuns were drowned—Hopkins leaped to the task. "The Wreck of the *Deutschland*" is a long and difficult poem that did not win favor for Hopkins, but it was the prototype of all his further work, both in terms of technique and of its resolute logics and celebrations within the framework of his faith. From his rigorous interpretation of Christianity—that sacrifice is bliss, and self-indulgence is the real death—Hopkins never wavered. His one escape from a life of self-restraint, labor, and humility was his feeling for the natural world—landscapes and waterways and copses, and especially the yearly gift of spring—in which he read the proof of God. Here, only, he could "merely" rejoice.* The results are the poems we know and love: the amazing lyrics of passion and thanks, in which there is neither meditation nor questions but, always, an exhilarating commitment. They are prayers, they are ornaments. They are rejoicements.

A Hopkins poem, like a Frost poem, is unmistakable. Its tone, diction, rhythm, etc., have a reliable "signature." Unlike Frost's work, where the diction is so miraculously akin to speech, Hopkins's poems are not natural sounding at all. Hopkins desired a real difference from usual speech or writing, and avoided both metrical formation of lines and diction that would resemble consistent natural expression. He did not want his poems to be mistaken for anything other than fervent, opulent declarations, elevated from the ordinary world; not on the nerves of questions do they exist, but with the candles, the breathy rhetoric, the pomp of certainty.

Hopkins dedicated many hours to a description and ex-

---

*One would like to say, Here, at least, he could relax. But "relax" is far too free and easy a word ever to use with Hopkins.

planation of his technique, whose mainstay was "sprung rhythm" and whose apparatus included such phrases as "hangers" and "outriders." Practically speaking, it is accentual verse and follows the course of logical intonation. There may be four or there may be five stresses to a line, and there are times when, to make this happen, one must compress a combination of words within a single emphasis, which adds to the density of the whole. The truth of the matter is that the poems do not require half the explanation Hopkins gave them, and to tell a further truth, he elaborates in such detail that it becomes finally obstacle rather than assistance. The poems are not hard to read. In their own way they are fluid, with obvious points of emphasis. There are unexpected lapses and ties and conjunctions within the syntax, but even with such moments the poems are readable and understandable. Also, as almost all poems do, they will occasionally, for a brief spell, make use of some familiar metrical pattern, that oldest obtainment of design.

If the explanations are overdone, still the form itself worked for Hopkins. Meditations, moving toward an answer, may well profit from simple language and a definite, reliable pattern, so that the reader may absorb carefully every step in the argument. Praise poems require no such step-by-step apparatus, but may come to the reader as they are felt by the writer — in a rush, in a spray, in a tumble and gallop, a pressure, a fulsomeness, an abundance, the sharp hooves of happiness lifting and flashing. A Hopkins poem is unmistakably joyful:

I walk, I lift up, I lift up heart, eyes,
    Down all that glory in the heavens to glean our Saviour....

But every life—even a short life, as Hopkins's life was—is full of pitfalls. The Hopkins we know best is the man who wrote "The Windhover" and "Hurrahing in Harvest" and "God's Grandeur." But Hopkins was also a man in turmoil. No doubt, as he put tremendous energy into each poem, he put a vast vocational energy into prayer and the various services he was called upon to perform. No doubt his daily faith was a deeply layered light. God, Christ, and Mary are ever in his poems, discovered and rediscovered out of some earthy, emblematic form. Still, even the most faithful man is in some sense passive, for a man receives grace and cannot make his own fortune altogether. It is in grace that one lives, or in hell—hell being, for a man of faith, that place, or those days, when the presence of God is withdrawn.

And such a trial and forlornness came to Hopkins. The energy with which he wrote his poems failed him. The presence of God withdrew from him. He wrote, during this time, what we now call his "terrible sonnets," and terrible they surely are. In his desolation he wrote them, and in an unusually simple diction; not with his usual long, jointless sentences but with the cramped and hinged hesitations of misery. If the praise poems seem sometimes like oversweet cake, these sonnets are the driest crusts.

Hopkins's nature was to live at either leaden depth or tumultuous height. This was certainly good for the poems, whose lavish density and upsweeps into exaltation create a world rarefied and glorious.

It is not unreasonable to imagine the intensity of Hopkins—Hopkins the poet, who was also Hopkins the religious—as the wish to transcend the mere words that listed the earth-evidences of God, and to merge with him completely. Such is the fierce desire of the mystic — impossible, yet ever present. Men live with it, as best they can.

Such men, and women too, do not of course need to be religious in the conventional sense (abiding, that is, by established tenets); many of them are not. For those who are, however, there is this difference: the nonreligious mystic generally has nothing to "work with" but intuition in the attempt to move nearer to creator, or mystical center, however one may define this core. While the religious person, a member of this or that church, this or that order, has a liturgy, a rule, an exact and exacting prescription of how to live, and what to do, and what not to do, in order to evolve a closeness — to *earn* a closeness — to God. Of all the religious orders, none is more rigorous than the Society of Jesus. The discipline of the Jesuits, their abstinence, their labors, are all severe. Indeed, Hopkins admitted that he found it a difficult life.

But my point is not simply that Hopkins found it difficult; rather, that in such a severe "program" of religious life there was every indication that nearness to God could be brought about by increasingly rigorous behavior, *more* prayer, *more* work, *more* abstinence. It was Loyola's way, and Hopkins chose it, and it wore him to the bone. That such behavior, born in humility, finally becomes a kind of self-exploitation rather than self-mastery, and therefore is no longer humility at all, of course complicates the issue. Hopkins, in the last years of his life, could not hide his weariness. At the age of forty-five he contracted typhoid fever, and it killed him.

For the poems that sprang so generously from Hopkins's mind we are deeply grateful. We are grateful also that, slowly, his forsakenness lifted, and in his final years he felt himself surrounded again by the light of heaven; he felt his "very-violet-sweet" God had returned. Indeed, his last poems seem, by comparison with the rest of his work, full of breath, confident, less afraid of uncertainty, almost stately. At last! "I am so happy, so happy," he said just before he died.

Hurrahing in Harvest

Summer ends now; now, barbarous in beauty, the stooks rise
   Around; up above, what wind-walks! what lovely behaviour
   Of silk-sack clouds! has wilder, wilful-wavier
Meal-drift moulded ever and melted across skies?

I walk, I lift up, I lift up heart, eyes,
   Down all that glory in the heavens to glean our Saviour;
   And, eyes, heart, what looks, what lips yet gave you a
Rapturous love's greeting of realer, of rounder replies?

And the azurous hung hills are his world-wielding shoulder
   Majestic—as a stallion stalwart, very-violet-sweet!—
These things, these things were here and but the beholder
   Wanting; which two when they once meet,
The heart rears wings bold and bolder
   And hurls for him, O half hurls earth for him off under his feet.

Gerard Manley Hopkins

Some Thoughts on Whitman

I

In *The Varieties of Religious Experience,* William James offers four marks of distinction that are part of a mystical experience. The first of these is that such an experience "defies expression, that no adequate report of its contents can be given in words."*

All poets know such frustration generally; the goal of creative work is ever approachable yet unattainable. But Whitman as he worked on *Leaves of Grass* may have been grappling with a more splendid difficulty than the usual—there is in his work a sense of mystical thickness and push, and a feeling that the inner man was at work under some exceptional excitement and compulsion. Whether Whitman had an actual mystical experience or not,† his was a sensibility so passionate, so affirmative and optimistic, that it is fair to speak of him as writing out of a kind of hovering mystical cloud. Clearly his idea of paradise was here—this hour and this place. And yet he was, in his way, just as the mystic is, a man of difference—a man apart.

James's other marks of distinction concerning the mystical experience are as follows, and also feel much in accord with the

---

*From *The Varieties of Religious Experience,* in *William James: Writings, 1902–1910* (New York: Library of America, 1987). The particular phrases quoted can be found on pp. 343–344.

†Ibid., p. 357.

emanations of *Leaves of Grass:* that mystical states "are illuminations, revelations…and as a rule they carry with them a curious sense of authority for after time"; that such a state "cannot be sustained for long"; and that the mystic feels "as if his own will were in abeyance, and indeed sometimes as if he were grasped and held by a superior power."

Whitman published *Leaves of Grass* in 1855, twelve poems and a prologue which unite into a single work. For the rest of his writing life Whitman wrote no other verse but fed it into that ever-expanding book—that is, all the work of his "after life" was refinement, addition, inculcation. Except in the hope of better effect, he took up no new subjects, nor altered the rhapsodic tenor of his voice, nor denied any effort of catalogue, rhetoric, eroticism, nor trimmed his cadence, nor muted his thunder or his sweetness. His message was clear from the first and never changed: that a better, richer life is available to us, and with all his force he advocated it both for the good of each individual soul and for the good of the universe.

That his methods are endlessly suggestive rather than demonstrative, and that their main attempt was to move the reader toward response rather than reflection, is perhaps another clue to the origin of Whitman's power and purpose, and to the weight of the task. If it is true that he experienced a mystical state, or even stood in the singe of powerful mystical suggestion, and James is right, then he was both blessed and burdened—for he could make no adequate report of it. He could only summon, suggest, question, call, and plead. And *Leaves of Grass* is indeed a sermon, a manifesto, a utopian document, a social contract, a political statement, an invitation, to each of us, to change. All through the poem we feel Whitman's persuading force, which is his sincerity; and we feel what the poem tries continually to be: the replication of a miracle.

2

The prose "Preface" that stands before the poems is wide-ranging and pontifical. Emerson lives here in both thought and word; actual phrases taken from Emerson's essays "The American Scholar" and "The Poet" are nailed down as Whitman's own. Whitman claims for his work the physical landscape and spiritual territory of America; in so doing he turns, like Emerson, from the traditions of Europe. He claims also, for the poet, a mental undertaking that is vast and romantic, and a seriousness that is close to divine.

The twelve poems of the 1855 edition of *Leaves of Grass* consist of one huge and gleaming Alp followed by a relaxed undulation of easily surmountable descending foothills. The initial poem, "Song of Myself" (sixty-two pages*), is the longest and the most critical. It is the Alp. If the reader can "stay with" this extended passage, he has made a passage indeed. The major demands of the poem are here established, the first and essential lesson given in the first half-dozen lines:

> I celebrate myself,
> And what I assume you shall assume,

---

*The number of pages devoted to this poem in *Walt Whitman: Complete Poetry and Collected Prose* (New York: Library of America, 1982).

For every atom belonging to me as good belongs to you.

I loafe and invite my soul,
I lean and loafe at my ease.... observing a spear of summer
    grass.   (p. 27)

In these lines the great work is begun, and the secret of success has been given. And what is that great labor? Out-circling interest, sympathy, empathy, transference of focus from the self to all else; the merging of the lonely single self with the wondrous, never-lonely entirety. This is all. The rest is literature: words, words, words; example, metaphor, narrative, lyricism, sweetness, persuasion, the stress of rhetoric, the weight of catalogue. The detail, the pace, the elaborations are both necessary and augmentative; this is a long poem and it is not an argument but a thousand examples, a thousand taps and twirls on Whitman's primary statement. Brevity would have made the whole thing ineffectual, for what Whitman is after is felt experience. Experience only, he understands, is the successful persuader.

Logic and sermons never convince,
The damp of the night drives deeper into my soul   (p. 56)

he says, and what would be prolongation or hyperbole in another man's book is part of the earnest and necessary equipage here.

The reader of *Leaves of Grass,* in this first section especially, is a major player, and is invited into this "theater of feeling" tenderly. "Song of Myself" is sprinkled with questions; toward the end of the poem they come thick and fast, their profusion, their slantness, their unanswerability helping the reader to rise out of familiar territory and into this soul-waking and world-shifting experience:

> Have you reckoned a thousand acres much? Have you
>   reckoned the earth much?   (p. 28)

> What do you think has become of the young and old men?
>   (p. 32)

> Who need be afraid of the merge?   (p. 33)

> The souls moving along.... are they invisible while the
>   least atom of the stones is visible?   (p. 34)

> Oxen that rattle the yoke or halt in the shade, what is that
>   you express in your eyes?   (p. 37)

> What is a man anyhow? What am I? and what are you?
>   (p. 45)

> Shall I pray? Shall I venerate and be ceremonious?   (p. 45)

and on and on. More than sixty questions in all, and not one of them easily answerable.

Nor, indeed, are they presented for answers, but to force open the soul:

> Unscrew the locks from the doors!
> Unscrew the doors themselves from their jambs!   (p. 50)

"Song of Myself" presents Whitman's invitation in a tone without margins — ecstasy, mysticism, urgency, seducements, open arms, and all those questions leave the reader plundered, exalted, and exhausted.

.   .   .

And so, amazingly, begins the long descent. The eleven poems remaining are various in tone and intention. In comparison with the sixty-two pages of "Song of Myself," each is surprisingly brief. In each section the author of "Song of Myself" continues to speak, but more comfortably, less extensively, less urgently, and at an increasing emotional distance from us.

Two of the poems are eleven pages long, another two are seven pages in length,* the last seven are all four pages long or less. If "The Sleepers" is almost palpably caressing, if "There Was a Child Went Forth" is flawlessly tender, if "A Boston Ballad" stands in its place with a surprising theatricality, still none of them measures anywhere near "Song of Myself," with its thunder and its kisses and its implications. So hot is the fire of that poem, so bright its transformative power, that we truly need, and Whitman knew it, each of the slow, descending chords that follow. There is a madness born of too much light, and Whitman was not after madness nor even recklessness, but the tranquility of affinity and function. He was after a joyfulness, a belief in existence in which man's inner light is neither rare nor elite, but godly and common, and acknowledged. For that it was necessary to be rooted, again, in the world.

3

One day as I wrestled with that long opening poem, the complaint burst from me: With Whitman it's opera, opera, opera all the time! I shouted, in something very like weariness.

---

*Poem length is taken from the volume previously cited.

It is true. For long stretches Whitman's tone of summoning and import is unalleviated. But it is necessary to his purpose, which is so densely serious. Neither whimsy nor the detailed and opulent level of fun-terror, as Poe for example employs it, is found in Whitman. Poe understood the usefulness of entertainment and employed it, although he too was dead serious. Whitman did not, nor even the expansions of narrative. In "Song of Myself" and in passages beyond as well are page after page of portrait and instance; each opens in a blink and shuts on another. They are not stories; they are glances, possibilities. They are any of us, almost, in another life, and they expect of the reader a costly exchange; we cannot glide here upon narrative but must imaginatively take on other destinies:

> The pure contralto sings in the organloft,
> The carpenter dresses his plank....the tongue of his
>   foreplane whistles its wild ascending lisp....   (p. 39)

> The bride unrumples her white dress, the minutehand of the
>   clock moves slowly....   (p. 41)

> The pilot seizes the king-pin, he heaves down with a strong
>   arm...
> The deacons are ordained with crossed hands at the altar...
> The lunatic is carried at last to the asylum a confirmed
>   case....   (p. 39)

All are unforgettable, even, or especially:

> ...the little child that peeped in at the door and then drew
>   back and was never seen again....   (p. 78)

Along with such portraits and moments of quickness and essence, Whitman turned upon the least detail of the manifest world such a fussy and diligent attention that the long lines lay down not so much ethereal as palpable. These lines with their iambic cadence and their end stops are like speech, yet not quite. They lack what speech so readily has — an uncertainty, a modesty, a feeling of attempt toward expression rather than re-iterated exactitude. Which is what Whitman has in such abundance: certitude, and a centering clarity of the least object.

Still, for all its intensity, Whitman's work is grammatically reasonable and abides by established rules. Such grammar-stability, compared for example with the syntactical compressions risked by Hopkins, makes a poetic line that is understandable, supple, and reliable. Such reliability assists Whitman's capacity to stay mild, or to flare, as the need may be. His style is made up of many elements but is not complex. The tones are various: vatic, tender, patriotic, journalistic, impassioned, avuncular, sensual. Insistence and excess are not naturally virtues, but Whitman makes them virtues in the service of his purpose.

Certain understandings still slip the search: how does the tender not become mincing? How does authority avoid pomp? How does cadence repeated and repeated summon rather than lull?

Most writing implies a distant, possible, even probable audience of a few or of many. *Leaves of Grass* assumes an intimate audience of one — one who listens closely to the solitary speaker. That is, to each reader the poem reaches out personally. It is mentoring, it is concerned; it is intimate. It contains the voice of the teacher and the preacher too, but it extends beyond their range. "Touch is the miracle," Whitman wrote in one of his workbooks. The words, in the long lines of *Leaves of Grass,* as near as words can be, are a spiritual and a physical touching.

4

A great loneliness was Whitman's constant companion, his prod, his necessary Other. One sees it everywhere in his personal life, his professional life, his beautifying portrayals of young men, his intense and prolonged references to the body's joy. It is supposed that a writer writes what he knows about and knows well. It is not necessarily so. A writer's subject may just as well, if not more likely, be what the writer longs for and dreams about, in an unquenchable dream, in lush detail and harsh honesty. Thus Whitman: grown man, lonely man. Sexual longing is the high note in the funneled-forth music of easy companionship with carriage drivers, sailors, wharf roughs, loose male energy, electric and swaggering. What else can we say? What else can we know? That it was not a trivial loneliness, or a passing loneliness, or a body loneliness only, but a loneliness near fatal.

> The sleepers are very beautiful as they lie unclothed,
> They flow hand in hand over the whole earth from east to
>   west as they lie unclothed.... (p. 115)

The fetch of his breath and the fetch of his ambition began on the shores of this loneliness. Without it he might have relaxed back from the endless and fiery work. He might have let a little moderation into his rhapsody. Certainly he would not have been the Whitman we mean when we say: the poet, Whitman.

> Darkness you are gentler than my lover....his flesh was
>   sweaty and panting,
> I feel the hot moisture yet that he left me.   (p. 109)

The erotic and the mystical are no strangers: each is a tempest; each drowns the individual in the yearn and success of combination; each calls us forth from an ordinary life to a new measure. For Whitman the erotic life of the body was all that the word "erotic" means, plus more; it was also its own music, its authority, and its manner of glazing our surroundings so that it seems we have been given new sight. James's four marks of distinction concerning mystical experience might apply without contortion to the erotic life as well. And Whitman, advocating the affirmative life of the body—I want to say the luster of the body—was at the same time in an alliance with the power of transformation. Was Whitman a mystic? For myself, I cannot answer the question except to say that surely he was a religious poet in the same sense that Emerson was a religious man, for whom life itself was light. For Emerson, it was light as clear as spring in his own orchard. For Whitman, it was that hot burning, that heaviness of intent, that vertigo, that trembling: that merge.

Eroticism is, both as eroticism exactly and as metaphor, what *Leaves of Grass* advocates: the healthy, heavy, seeded life of the soul. That such advocacy brought him criticism no doubt was disappointing, but he did not change his work. That he was called coarse and rank must have dismayed him, but he did not alter anything. There was no way he could delete or dilute this part of his cosmology. It was central to everything he wanted to say.

> To be surrounded by beautiful curious breathing laughing
>   flesh is enough,
> To pass among them.. to touch any one.... to rest my arm
>   ever so lightly round his or her neck for a moment
>   ....what is this then?
> I do not ask any more delight.... I swim in it as in a sea.
>   (p. 120)

5

What cannot be told can be suggested; such is the theater of *Leaves of Grass,* hugely long, opulent, illustrative, intense, oracular, tender, luxurious. And you must take it to the hilt, you must stay with it almost beyond endurance, for

> This is the grass that grows wherever the land is and the
>   water is,
> This is the common air that bathes the globe.   (p. 43)

Of all American poems, the 1855 *Leaves of Grass* is the most probable of effect upon the individual sensibility. It wants no less. We study it as literature, but like all great literature it has a deeper design: it would be a book for men to live by. It is obsessively affirmative. It is foolishly, childishly, obsessively affirmative. It offers a way to live, in the religious sense, that is intelligent and emotive and rich, and dependent only on the individual—no politics, no liturgy, no down payment. Just: attention, sympathy, empathy. Neither does Whitman speak of hell or damnation; rather, he is parental and coaxing, tender and provocative in his drawing us toward him. Line by line, he amalgamates to the fact. Brawn and spirit, we are built of light, and God is within us. This is the message of his long, honeyed harangue. This is the absolute declaration, and this is the verifying experience of his poem.

> Swift wind! Space! My Soul! Now I know it is true what I
> > guessed at;
> What I guessed when I loafed on the grass,
> What I guessed while I lay alone in my bed....and again
> > as I walked the beach under the paling stars of the
> > morning.   (p. 59)

PART THREE

Intermission

The Boat

1

I think a great deal about Shelley's boat, a little world sailing upon the greater world, to whose laws it must, of necessity, submit. As we know, it soon carried Shelley to his death, and his friend Edward Williams and the boy Charles Vivian as well. The details we do not know, whether it was the wind mainly or altogether, or the leafy waves, or the wind and the waves together, or a larger boat bearing down through the sudden storm. But this we do know. Before it happened, I mean when they left land and sailed away over the Aegean, in the clear summer air, on the untroubled sea, the boat must have looked like a white bird, a swan, floating so lightly and rapidly it was all but flying. And sailing in it must have seemed like entering, with justifiable exhilaration and total faith, an even larger, lovelier, statelier and steadier world than the manifest ocean. As, perhaps, it was.

2

There are as many worlds as there are imaginers. Down-shore there rests in the restless water a sailboat; one line holds it from leaping away. Little bell, little chain, little this and that, on it, taps and clanks in the wind. I stand and listen. Its bow, built of boards steamed to a sweet curve and join, like a bird's breast, tugs against the line. What is it it wants to be? Once, in Union, Maine, as we were passing a field, five white birch trees became five white ponies. Their feet shuffled in the long grass, their white faces shone. This is called: happiness. This is called: stay away from me with your inches, and your savings accounts, and your plums in a jar. Your definitive anything. And if life is so various, so shifting, what could we possibly say of death, that black leaf, that has in it any believable finality?

Sand Dabs, Four*

She said, "The fox hunt is good for the fox."
"Which fox?" I said.

❧

Try to live through one day believing nothing is significant, nothing is governed by the unknowable, the divine. See how you feel by the end of such a day.

❧

What is called definitive is, right away, a brag.

❧

The arena of *things,* the theater of the *imagination,* the everywhere of *faith.*

❧

When men sell their souls, where do the souls go?

❧

In order to be the person I want to be, I must strive, hourly, against the drag of the others.

❧

Every day I think of Schubert and the mystery of his six hundred songs.

❧

What is spiritual about the manifest is not the part that leaves tracks in the snow.

---

*The first three "Sand Dabs" are in two previous books, *Blue Pastures* and *West Wind.* The sand dab is a small, bony, not very significant but well-put-together fish.

Sand Dabs, Five

What men build, in the name of security, is built of straw.

૭

Does the grain of sand
know it is a grain of sand?

૭

My dog Ben—a mouth like a tabernacle.

૭

You can have the other words—chance, luck, coincidence,
serendipity. I'll take grace. I don't know what it is exactly, but
I'll take it.

૭

The pine cone has secrets it will never tell.

૭

Myself, myself, myself, that darling hut!
How quick it will burn!

૭

Death listens
to the hum and strike of my words.
His laughter spills.

૭

Spring: there rises up from the earth such a blazing sweetness
it fills you, thank God, with disorder.

૭

I am a performing artist; I perform admiration.
Come with me, I want my poems to say. *And do the same.*

Sand Dabs, Six

Sweet Emerson—always passionate about ideas, always reasonable about passion.

୧୨

Nobody ever says of a painter that he has lost his way. It is said of writers. But when one is talking about a painter one says, "He is finding his way."

୧୨

In more than one book I have read that Blake was actually not very good at versification; in a like number of books, if not more, I have read that Swinburne was too good at it.

୧୨

As a carpenter can make a gibbet as well as an altar, a writer can describe the world as trivial or exquisite, as material or as idea, as senseless or as purposeful. Words are wood.

୧୨

I can think for a little while; then, it's the world again.

୧୨

The cranberry bog—its rim an old slop-happy red.

୧୨

Every word is a messenger. Some have wings; some are filled with fire; some are filled with death.

୧୨

For weeks the cut evergreens
shag a fragrance.

୧୨

And the thrush sings
like a finger of God.

Swoon

In a corner of the stairwell of this rented house a most astonishing adventure is going on. It is only the household of a common spider,* a small, rather chaotic web half in shadow. Yet it burgeons with the ambition of a throne. She—for it is the female that is always in sight—has produced six egg sacs, and from three of them, so far, an uncountable number of progeny have spilled. Spilled is precisely the word, for the size and the motions of these newborns are so meager that they appear at first utterly lifeless, as though the hour of beginning had come and would not be deferred, and thrust them out, with or without their will, to cling in a dark skein in the tangled threads.

I am less precise about the timing of these events than I would like. While I was quick to notice the spider and her web, I was slow to write down the happenings as they occurred, a concordance I now wish I had. It was so casual at first, I was sure that something—probably a careless motion on my part—would demolish or tear the web and remove the spider from sight. But it did not happen.

I began to watch her in October, and it's fair to say that,

---

*Probably *Theridium tepidariorum.*

being a poor sleeper especially when away from home, I have watched her quite as much during the night as during the day.

Now it is early December.

I am extremely careful as I descend or ascend the stairs.

Perhaps when I pass by she senses my heft and shadow. But she floats on her strings and does not move. Nor, I think, would she flee easily from any intrusion. Her egg sacs, all of them, are hanging near her, in an archipelago, the oldest at the top and the newest at the bottom, and without question she is attached to them in some bond of cherishing. Often she lies with her face against the most recently constructed, touching it with her foremost set of limbs. And why should she not be fond of it? She made it from the materials of her own body—deft and plump she circled and circled what was originally a small package, and caused it to grow larger as the thread flowed from her body. She wrapped and wrapped until, now, the sac sways with the others in the threads of the web, not round exactly, but like a Lilliputian gas balloon, pulled slightly along the vertical.

And still she fusses, pats it and circles it, as though coming to a judgment; then pats some more, or dozes, still touching it. Finally, she withdraws her sets of legs, curls them, almost as if in a swoon, or a death, and hangs, motionless, for a full half day. She seems to sleep.

The male spider comes and goes. Every third or fourth day I catch sight of him lurking at the edge of the web. What he eats I cannot guess, for the treasures of the web—which do not come, sometimes, for many days—are to all evidence for the female only. Whether she refuses to offer him a place at her table, or whether he has no need of it, I do not know. He is a dapper spider; being male and no spinner, he lacks the necessity of the pouch-like body in which to store the materials from which comes the bold and seemingly endless thread. He is therefore free to be of another nature altogether—small, and shy, and quick.

Twice while I have been watching, when the egg sacs have been in the unseeable process of pouring the tiny, billeted spiders forth, he has been in the web. Perhaps, like some male cats, and other mammals also, he will take this arrival with ill humor and feast on a few of his own progeny.

I do not know.

Whenever I see him poised there and lean closer to him, he steps briskly backward, is instantly enfolded into darkness and gone from sight.

It is five A.M.

Good fortune has struck the web like an avalanche. A cricket—not the black, flat-bodied, northern sort I am used to, but a paler variety, with a humped, shrimp-like body and whip-like antennae and jumper's legs—has become enmeshed in the web.

This spider is not an orb weaver; that is, she does not build a net silken and organized and centered along a few strong cables. No, her web is a poor thing. It is flung forth, ungloriously, only a few inches above the cellar floor. What is visible is in a wild disorder. Nevertheless, it functions; it holds, now, the six egg cases and the cricket, which struggles in a sort of sling of webbing.

The spider now is never still. She descends to the cricket again and again, then hastens away and hangs a short distance above. Though it is almost impossible to see, a fine line follows her, jetting from her spinneret; as she moves, she is wrapping the cricket. Soon the threads thicken; the cricket is bound with visible threads at the ankles, which keep it from tearing loose with the strength of the huge back legs. How does the spider know what it knows? Little by little the cricket's long front limbs with their serrated edges, flung in an outward gesture from its body, are also being wrapped. Soon the cricket's efforts to free itself are only occasional—a few yawings toward push or pull—then it is motionless.

All this has taken an hour.

There has been nothing consumable in the web for more than a week, during which time the spider has made her sixth egg case and, presumably, before that, carried through some motions of romance with her consort, and produced the actual eggs. Her body during this week—I mean that dust-colored, sofa-button, bulbous part of her body so visible to our eyes— has shrunk to half its previous size.

Then, as I continued to watch, the spider began a curious and coordinated effort. She dropped to the cricket and with her foremost limbs, which are her longest, she touched its body. The response was an immediate lurching of cricket, also spider and web. Swiftly she turned—she was, in fact, beginning the motions of turning even as she reached forward and then, even before the cricket reacted, with her hindmost pair of limbs she *kicked* it. She did this over and over—descending, touching and turning, kicking—each of her kicks targeting the cricket's stretched-out back limbs. She did this perhaps twenty times. With every blow the cricket swung, then rocked back to motionlessness, the only signs of life a small, continual motion of the jointed mouth, and a faint bubbling therefrom.

As I watched, the spider wrapped its thread again around the cricket's ankles. Then, with terrible and exact precision, she moved toward an indentation of flesh just at the elbow joint of the cricket's left front limb—and to this soft place she dipped her mouth. But, yet again, at this touch, the cricket lurched. So she retreated, and waited, and then again, with an undivertable aim, descended to that elbow where, finally, with no reaction from the cricket, she was able for perhaps three minutes to place her small face. There, as I imagine it, she began to infuse her flesh-dissolving venom into the channels of the cricket's body. Intermittently the cricket still moved, so this procedure even yet required some stopping and restarting, but it was clearly an unretractable operation. At length, in twenty minutes perhaps, the cricket lay utterly quiescent; and then the spider moved, with the most gentle and certain of motions, to the cricket's head, its bronze, visor-like face, and there, again surely and with no hesitation, the spider positioned her body, her mouth once more at some chosen juncture, near throat, the spinal cord, the brain.

Now she might have been asleep as she lay, lover-like, alongside the cricket's body. Later—hours later—she moved down along its bronze chest, and there fed again. Slowly her shrunken body grew larger, then very large. And then it was night.

· · ·

Early in the morning, the cricket was gone. As I learned from later examples, when the quiescent cricket was no more than a shell, she had cut it loose. It had dropped to the cellar floor, where any number of living crickets occasionally went leaping by. By any one of them it had been dragged away. Now the spider, engorged, was motionless. She slept with her limbs enfolded slightly—the same half clench of limbs one sees in the bodies of dead spiders—but this was the twilight rest, not the final one. This was the restoration, the interval, the sleep of the exhausted and the triumphant.

I have not yet described the mystery and enterprise for which she lives—the egg sacs and the young spiders. They emerge from their felt balloon and hang on threads near it: a fling, a nebula. Only by putting one's face very close, and waiting, and not breathing, can one actually see that the crowd is moving. It is motion not at all concerted or even definite but it is motion, and that, compared with no movement at all, is of course everything. And it grows. Perhaps the spiders feel upon the tender hairs of their bodies the cool, damp cellar air, and it is a lure. They want more. They want to find out things. The tiny limbs stretch and shuffle.

Little by little, one or two, then a dozen, begin to drift into a wider constellation—toward the floor or the stair wall—spreading outward even as the universe is said to be spreading toward the next adventure and the next, endlessly.

In six or seven days after their birth, the little spiders are gone. And my attention passes from that opened and shrunken pod to the next below it, which is still secretly ripening, in which the many minuscule bodies are still packed tightly together, like a single thing.

How do they get out of the egg sac? Do they tear it with their fragile limbs? Do they chew it with their unimaginably tiny mouths?

I do not know.

Nor do I know where they all go, though I can imagine the dispersal of thousands into the jaws of the pale, leaping crickets. Certainly only a few of them survive, or we would be awash upon their rippling exertions.

Only once in this space of time, after the bursting of three of the six pods, did I see what was clearly a young spider; many times its original birth size and still no larger than a pencil's point, it was crawling steadily away through a last hem of the mother web.

This is the moment in an essay when the news culminates and, subtly or bluntly, the moral appears. It is a music to be played with the lightest fingers. All the questions that the spider's curious life made me ask, I know I can find answered in some book of knowledge, of which there are many. But the palace of knowledge is different from the palace of discovery, in which I am, truly, a Copernicus. *The world is not what I thought, but different, and more! I have seen it with my own eyes!*

But a spider? Even that?

Even that.

Our time in this rented house was coming to an end. For days I considered what to do with the heroine of this story and her enterprise, or if I should do anything at all. The owners of the house were to return soon; no reason to think they would not immediately sweep her away. And, in fact, we had ordered a housecleaning directly following our departure. Should I attempt to move her, therefore? And if so, to what place? To the dropping temperatures of the yard, where surely she could not last out the coming winter? To another basement corner? But would the crickets be there? Would the shy male spider find her? Could I move the egg sacs without harming them, and the web intact, to hold them?

Finally, I did nothing. I simply was not able to risk wrecking her world, and I could see no possible way I could move the whole kingdom. So I left her with the only thing I could — the certainty of a little more time. For our explicit and stern instructions to the cleaners were to scrub the house — but to stay out of this stairwell altogether.

The Storm

Now through the white orchard my little dog
    romps, breaking the new snow
    with wild feet.
Running here running there, excited,
    hardly able to stop, he leaps, he spins
until the white snow is written upon
    in large, exuberant letters,
a long sentence, expressing
    the pleasures of the body in this world.

Oh, I could not have said it better
    myself.

PART FOUR

Winter Hours

Winter Hours

I

IN THE WINTER I am writing about, there was much darkness. Darkness of nature, darkness of event, darkness of the spirit. The sprawling darkness of *not knowing*. We speak of the light of reason. I would speak here of the darkness of the world, and the light of _____. But I don't know what to call it. Maybe hope. Maybe faith, but not a shaped faith — only, say, a gesture, or a continuum of gestures. But probably it is closer to hope, that is more active, and far messier than faith must be. Faith, as I imagine it, is tensile, and cool, and has no need of words. Hope, I know, is a fighter and a screamer.

Because my workday begins early, it begins, in winter, in the huge, tense blackness of the world.

The house is hard cold. Winter walks up and down the town swinging his censer, but no smoke or sweetness comes from it, only the sour, metallic frankness of salt and snow. I dress in the dark and hurry out. The sleepy dogs walk with me a few strides, then they disappear. The water slaps crisply upon the cold-firmed sand. I listen intently, as though it is a language the ocean is speaking. There are no stars, nor a moon. Still I can tell that the tide is rising, as it speaks singingly, and I can see a little from the street lamps and from the amber lights along the wharf. The water tosses its black laces and flaunts, streaked with the finest tain. Now and again the dogs come back, their happy feet dashing the sand. Before we reach the sea wall again, and cross the yard, it is no longer night. We stand by the door of the house. We stand upon the thin blue peninsula that leads to the sharp, white day. A small black cat bounds from under the rose bushes; the dogs bark joyfully.

This is the beginning of every day.

I have never been to Rome. I have never been to Paris, or Greece, or Sweden, or India. I went once to England, so long ago it seems like the Middle Ages. M. and I went once to the Far East, Japan and Malaysia and New Zealand and Indonesia, and I am glad I saw the Southern Cross, but I have not forgotten how it felt to think I was going to fall off the planet. I am not a traveler. Not of that sort.

I do know the way to the grocery store, and I can get that far. The simples of our lives: bread, fruit, vegetables. In the big store. The old small stores, with which I was long familiar, are gone. Though there are new ones, to suit new purposes. Previously there were small shops because it was a small town. Now there are small shops because the tourists want to think they are still in that little town, which has vanished. It is good business now to appear antiquated, with narrow aisles and quaintly labeled jars.

From the oldest resource of all, the sea, still comes food, occasionally, by hook or by chance. One morning I find three fish on the beach as fresh as young celery—cod, each of them a little over a foot long. I bring them home. The largest of the three has been gaffed, so it is apparent the fish came from the wharf, having escaped some packing crate or boat. The three fish have made their landfall close together, which bespeaks the purposeful motions of the tide as it laps toward shore. The fish are exquisite, with torpedo-shaped bodies, dark speckles under a sea-green glaze, hard heads with a fleshy jaw appendage, large eyes. They have many small cutting teeth, but by no means like those of the more aggressive bluefish. Neither is there any sudden place along the spine where the hand, unaware, could be badly tapped or torn, as there is on the body of the bluefish.

I clean the fish and call M. to come and see the insides of the last one, before I scoop the ship of its body to a smooth emptiness. The many shapes and shades of pink are astounding — the heart, the frillery and drapery of the lungs, the swim bladder, the large liver. The tongue in the wide mouth, pale and fat, is like the tongue of a newborn pug.

In fact, there is something called tongues and cheeks in the fish shops. Now I see on each head two areas, the size of half-dollars, where I might have lifted out a fine plug of flesh, and gone a-chowdering. Instead I take the heads, spines, etc., out to the beach, in a blue pail, and dump them on an influx of sand. A few gulls in the distance cry out and are there almost on the instant, on one wing-pull. They make quick work of all of it, in the pink-tipped late afternoon light.

The fish are delicious.

For years when the tide was high I went, early or late, to another part of the world, which is mostly pinewoods. What you imagine when I say "pine" might not be our variety, which is also called pitch pine, or scrub pine. It is a modest tree, twisty and aromatic. It can live in the face of the sea wind, giving up its chances for girth and height, perhaps, for valuable elasticity. There are black oaks also, and tupelos that tend to set down roots in the dampness along the edges of the ponds.

Through these woods I have walked thousands of times. For many years I felt more at home here than anywhere else, including our own house. Stepping out into the world, into the grass, onto the path, was always a kind of relief. I was not escaping anything. I was returning to the arena of delight. I was stepping across some border. I don't mean just that the world changed the other side of the border, but that I did too. Eventually I began to appreciate—I don't say this lightly—that the great black oaks knew me. I don't mean they knew me as myself and not another—that kind of individualism was not in the air—but that they recognized and responded to my presence, and to my mood. They began to offer, or I began to feel them offer, their serene greeting. It was like a quick change of temperature, a warm and comfortable flush, faint yet palpable, as I walked toward them and beneath their outflowing branches.

In the pinewoods is where the owl floats, and where the white egret paces, in summer, like a winged snake, in the flashing shallows. Here is where two deer approached me one morning, in an unforgettable sweetness, their faces like light brown flowers, their eyes kindred and full of curiosity. The mouth of one of them, and its vibrant tongue, touched my hand. This is where the coyotes appeared, one season, and followed me, bold beyond belief, and nimble—lean ferocities just held in check. This is where, once, I heard suddenly a powerful beating of wings, a feisty rhythm, a pomp of sound, within it a thrust then a slight uptake. The wings of angels might sound so, who are after all not mild but militant, and cross the skies on important missions. Then, just above the trees, their feet trailing and their eyes blazing, two swans flew by.

The world changes. Now the entrance to the pinewoods is closed and barred at night, at least in the warm seasons, and one may not enter until this barrier is moved back, which happens hours past sunrise. And any day of the year, dogs are banned, or must walk, leashed, along a single designated path. The rangers carry firearms and handcuffs and ride squat vehicles over the dunes or past the twisty pine groves. They are looking for trouble: running dogs, campers, lovers, someone with a handful of flowers or a pail of cranberries; someone who has moved the barrier aside and come in, to stroll updune in time to see the sun float into the world, pink rose of peace, from the dark horizon. They shall be found, and they will be fined, and chastised.

Of course I know a path or two where I can sneak in, to the owl and the snow and the sunrise. But I do it less and less. It's not the fine but the apprehension that has ruined my visitation, which was such a deep excitement and such a serious part of my life and my writing. Pleasure was my text; how could I contrive pleasure where I have become the hunted?

There is a place in the woods, though, where the vanishing bodies of our dogs, our dogs of the past, lie in the sweet-smelling earth. How they ran through these woods! Too late, world, to deny them their lives of motion, of burly happiness.

After Luke died, I crossed and recrossed the Province-lands, wherever we had been, and wherever I found her pawprints in the sand I dragged branches and leaves and slabs of bark over them, so they would last, would keep from the wind a long time. Then, overnight, after maybe three weeks, in a dazzling, rearranging rain, they were gone.

Morning, for me, is the time of best work. My conscious thought sings like a bird in a cage, but the rest of me is singing too, like a bird in the wind. Perhaps something is still strong in us in the morning, the part that is untamable, that dreams willfully and crazily, that knows reason is no more than an island within us.

In the act of writing the poem, I am obedient, and submissive. Insofar as one can, I put aside ego and vanity, and even intention. I listen. What I hear is almost a voice, almost a language. It is a second ocean, rising, singing into one's ear, or deep inside the ears, whispering in the recesses where one is less oneself than a part of some single indivisible community. Blake spoke of taking dictation. I am no Blake, yet I know the nature of what he meant. Every poet knows it. One learns the craft, and then casts off. One hopes for gifts. One hopes for direction. It is both physical, and spooky. It is intimate, and inapprehensible. Perhaps it is for this reason that the act of first-writing, for me, involves nothing more complicated than paper and pencil. The abilities of a typewriter or computer would not help in this act of slow and deep listening.

I could not be a poet without the natural world. Someone else could. But not me. For me the door to the woods is the door to the temple. Under the trees, along the pale slopes of sand, I walk in an ascendant relationship to rapture, and with words I celebrate this rapture. I see, and dote upon, the manifest.

Persons environmentally inclined have suggested that I am one of them. I don't argue with them, but it's not quite a fit. My work doesn't document any of the sane and learned arguments for saving, healing, and protecting the earth for our existence. What I write begins and ends with the act of noticing and cherishing, and it neither begins nor ends with the human world. Maybe I would be an environmentalist if I thought about it. But I don't. I don't think in terms of the all, the network of our needs and our misdeeds, the interrelationship of our lives and the lives of all else. On the contrary, I am forever just going out for a walk and tripping over the root, or the petal, of some trivia, then seeing it as if in a second sight, as emblematic. By no means is this a unique way to live but is, rather, the path found by all who are mystically inclined.

Further, the world makes a great distinction between kinds of life: human on the one hand, all else on the other hand. Or it throws everything into two categories: animate, and inanimate. Which are neither of them distinctions I care about. The world is made up of cats, and cattle, and fenceposts! A chair is alive. The blue bowl of the pond, and the blue bowl on the table, that holds six apples, are all animate, and have spirits. The coat, the paper clip, the shovel, as well as the lively rain-dappled grass, and the thrush singing his gladness, and the rain itself. What are divisions for, if you look into it, but to lay out a stratification — that is, to suggest where an appreciative or not so appreciative response is proper, to each of the many parts of our indivisible world?

What I want to describe in my poems is the nudge, the

prick of the instant, the flame of appreciation that shoots from my heels to my head when compass grass bends its frilled branches and draws a perfect circle on the cold sand; or when the yellow wasp comes, in fall, to my wrist and then to my plate, to ramble the edges of a smear of honey.

There is nothing so special in this, I know. Neither does it prove anything. But living like this is for me the difference between a luminous life and a ho-hum life. So be it! With my whole heart, I live as I live. My affinity is to the whimsical, the illustrative, the suggestive — not to the factual or the useful. I walk, and I notice. I am sensual in order to be spiritual. I look into everything without cutting into anything. And then I come home and M. says — she always says it! — *How was it?* The answer has never varied or been less than spontaneous: *It was wonderful.*

M. and I met in the late fifties. For myself it was all adolescence again — shivers and whistles. Certainty. We have lived together for more than thirty years, so far. I would not tell much about it. Privacy, no longer cherished in the world, is all the same still a natural and sensible attribute of paradise. We are happy, and we are lucky. We are neither political nor inclined to likecompany. Repeat: we are happy, and we are lucky. We make for each other: companionship, intimacy, affection, rhapsody. Whenever I hear of something horrible, I want to cover M.'s ears. Whenever I see something beautiful, and my heart is shouting, it is M. I run to, to tell about it.

When I write about nature directly, or refer to it, here are some things I don't mean, and a few I do. I don't mean nature as ornamental, however scalloped and glowing it may be. I don't mean nature as useful to man if that possibility of utility takes from an object its own inherent value. Or, even, diminishes it. I don't mean nature as calamity, as vista, as vacation or recreation. I don't mean landscapes in which we find rest and pleasure — although we do — so much as I mean landscapes in which we are reinforced in our sense of the world as a mystery, a mystery that entails other privileges besides our own — and also, therefore, a hierarchy of right and wrong behaviors pertaining to that mystery, diminishing it or defending it.

The man who does not know nature, who does not walk under the leaves as under his own roof, is partial and wounded. I say this even as wilderness shrinks beneath our unkindnesses and our indifference. Nature there will always be, but it will not be what we have now, much less the deeper fields and woodlands many of us remember from our childhood. The worlds of van Gogh and Turner and Winslow Homer, and Wordsworth too, and Frost and Jeffers and Whitman, are gone, and will not return. We can come to our senses yet, and rescue the world, but we will never return it to anything like its original form.

When I came to a teachable age, I was, as most youngsters are, directed toward the acquisition of knowledge, meaning not so much ideas but demonstrated facts. Education as I knew it was made up of such a preestablished collection of certainties.

Knowledge has entertained me and it has shaped me and

it has failed me. Something in me still starves. In what is probably the most serious inquiry of my life, I have begun to look past reason, past the provable, in other directions. Now I think there is only one subject worth my attention and that is the recognition of the spiritual side of the world and, within this recognition, the condition of my own spiritual state. I am not talking about having faith necessarily, although one hopes to. What I mean by spirituality is not theology, but attitude. Such interest nourishes me beyond the finest compendium of facts. In my mind now, in any comparison of demonstrated truths and unproven but vivid intuitions, the truths lose.

I would therefore write a kind of elemental poetry that doesn't just avoid indoors but doesn't even *see* the doors that lead inward—to laboratories, to textbooks, to knowledge. I would not talk about the wind, and the oak tree, and the leaf on the oak tree, but on their behalf. I would talk about the owl and the thunderworm and the daffodil and the red-spotted newt as a company of spirits, as well as bodies. I would say that the fox stepping out over the snow has nerves as fine as mine, and a better courage. I would write praise poems that might serve as comforts, reminders, or even cautions if needed, to wayward minds and unawakened hearts.

I would say that there exist a thousand unbreakable links between each of us and everything else, and that our dignity and our chances are one. The farthest star and the mud at our feet are a family; and there is no decency or sense in honoring one thing, or a few things, and then closing the list. The pine tree, the leopard, the Platte River, and ourselves—we are at risk together, or we are on our way to a sustainable world together. We are each other's destiny.

3

We hear on the forecast that it may snow, or it may rain, and there will be high wind. Certainly there is wind. The rest passes out to sea, but the wind is sufficient. Clap of invisible hands and all the winds together, those breezy brothers, they are on their way.

The storm comes on an incoming tide; it therefore grows in power for the six hours of flashing tumble and shove toward us. The wind is from the south-southwest. The fetch, then— that length of open water in the path of the storm—is the distance of the bay, across the water. A distance great enough to roughen even the basins of the ocean waters here, and to swell mightily the power of the waves. Indeed, what such fetch and wind in the rising tide do to the water of the surface is beautiful and dreadful. It shines, for the clouds are thin and racing by, and the light alters from gray to steel to a terrible flashing, a shirred, swarming surface. Sometimes, in summer, the water seems not only to catch and reprise the sun's light, but to contain light of its own making, that rises from below. Not now. Now it is all darkness that rises, to meet this frieze of surface waves, the random creases and spreads of light. It is sharp, it is painfully bright, mirror bright, mercurial and flowing and molten. What could live, now, in the interpourings below, or on the raked surface? The eiders, hour after hour, bounce and dive and emerge with small fish and crabs. For them the roughness means disruption below, in which many nourishing tidbits may be found—crabs risen from the sand, fish separated from their tumbling schools. The eiders' high-set eyes are cheerful. The black ducks, though, that love sunshine and low tide, have vanished. And most of the gulls, those that still coast by, are in some peril, for they must aim through the wind; pull as they may on their strong wings, they cannot plow a chosen way, but must sink and dodge the black rocks of the groins, and the roofs of the buildings nearest the water.

The wind pounds. It can't be pounding, there is nothing to pound, no opposition, just molten slabs of water as ocean rolls its bales of brightness to the shore where they smash hugely, row after row. Yet it is the pounding of the wind that one hears. Fences creak and flap, doorways whistle, loose objects thump down or fly off porches, or roll down beach. But the noise of loosening and rolling is as nothing compared to the outpouring, the lashing and whistling from both above and below, ocean and sky-loft both. It is a many-layered choir; the sopranos shriek, the altos follow in disharmony, the chesty tenors and baritones fling out their notes of brass. The basses make great black O's of their lips, and simply, unceasingly, exhale. The ranks of the waves—dark, white-bearded, and sand-filled as they roll in their turn up the beach and toward us—never hurry, never hesitate, never stop coming. For hours it continues: still dreadful, still beautiful. It is frightening too, fraught with peril for anything so minor as a house, or so breakable as a human person.

Sometimes the surface takes on a tarnished glow, as it heaves and throws the white spume skyward. One could be standing in the same place, by the same sea, a thousand years ago. In spite of the motion and the noise, that glow releases something strangely peaceful. It is not unlike the calm that one reaches in the deepest influence of great art, where the spirit senses that purest of mysteries: power without anger, injury without malice. For nature and art are in this way twins: they are both beautiful, and dreadful, and in love with change.

Then, it is close to high tide. A small blue boat appears, bumping the sea wall. A forlorn sight. One can hardly believe it is inanimate, it seems to strive so against collision, and to wince with each knock of the waves that sends it roughly against the wall. The bow turns and turns, as if in an effort to escape. It is swamped, and without hope. We could go out and perhaps get our hands on the dragging line. But we could not hold it against the storm's force. It lurches on, the west wind wild behind as it pitches to the east, bumping and bumping against the sea wall. Then it is out of sight.

Then the sea, at crest, a full flood, lifts itself; it flies, it enters the yard. Like long great silver draperies, with wide pleats opening and sizzling, the waves rise and shake themselves in bright flounces over the sea wall. The water is so loaded with sand that with each vanishing of the fallen wave the yard appears newly made. The sprawled waves erase all history — footprints, dog tracks, litter — it is all scoured and laid over with the cleanest grains.

So, at the sixth hour, the ocean arrives — and soaked the roses, and flung spray to the deck, and then it said, *Not this time*, and, still screaming, but with each wave a less dreadful scream, it began to descend.

4

So the storm passed, that one.

·   ·   ·

Sometimes I think, were I just a little rougher made, I would go altogether to the woods—to my work entirely, and solitude, a few friends, books, my dogs, all things peaceful, ready for meditation and industry—if for no other reason than to escape the heart-jamming damages and discouragements of the world's mean spirits. But, no use. Even the most solitudinous of us is communal by habit, and indeed by commitment to the bravest of our dreams, which is to make a moral world. The whirlwind of human behavior is not to be set aside.

Now comes a peaceful day, all day long. Then comes evil, crossing the street, going out of its way with determined steps and a face like a nail—invasive, wanting to molest, to hurt, to stain, to dismay, to dishearten. This is no discourse, I have not even the beginnings of sufficient knowledge to hunt down the reasons why. I suppose they, those lives soaked in evil, are miserable and so they ever despise happiness. I suppose they feel powerless and therefore must exert power wherever they can, which is so often upon those unable to comprehend what is happening, much less defend themselves.

Where does such a force come from? What does it mean? A voice very faint, and inside me, offers a possibility: how shall there be redemption and resurrection unless there has been a great sorrow? And isn't struggle and rising the real work of our lives? Maybe in ten more years I will have another idea. Meanwhile I know this: evil is one part of our beautiful world. And though my writing pays it small attention, I am not blinkered; I, too, have been forced to stand close to it, and have felt the almost muscular agony of impotence before it, unable to interfere or assuage or do anything effective.

Though I do — oh yes I do — believe the soul is improvable. Oh sweet and defiant hope!

5

"Put yourself in the way of grace," says a friend of ours, who is a monk, and a bishop; and he smiles his floating and shining smile.

And truly, can there be a subject of more interest to each of us than whether or not grace exists, and the soul? And, consequent upon the existence of the soul, a whole landscape of incorruptible forces, perhaps even a source, an almost palpably suggested second universe? A world that is incomprehensible through reason?

To believe in the soul — to believe in it exactly as much and as hardily as one believes in a mountain, say, or a fingernail, which is ever in view — imagine the consequences! How far-reaching, and thoroughly wonderful! For everything, by such a belief, would be charged, and changed. You wake in the morning, the soul exists, your mouth sings it, your mind accepts it. And the perceived, tactile world is, upon the instant, only half the world!

How easily I travel, about halfway, through such a scenario. I believe in the soul — in mine, and yours, and the bluejay's, and the pilot whale's. I believe each goldfinch flying away over the coarse ragweed has a soul, and the ragweed too, plant by plant, and the tiny stones in the earth below, and the grains of earth as well. Not romantically do I believe this, nor poetically, nor emotionally, nor metaphorically except as all reality is metaphor, but steadily, lumpishly, and absolutely.

The wild waste spaces of the sea, and the pale dunes with one hawk hanging in the wind, they are for me the formal spaces that, in a liturgy, are taken up by prayer, song, sermon, silence, homily, scripture, the architecture of the church itself.

And as with prayer, which is a dipping of oneself toward the light, there is a consequence of attentiveness to the grass itself, and the sky itself, and to the floating bird. I too leave the fret and enclosure of my own life. I too dip myself toward the immeasurable.

Now winter, the winter I am writing about, begins to ease. And what, if anything, has been determined, selected, nailed down? This is the lesson of age—events pass, things change, trauma fades, good fortune rises, fades, rises again but different. Whereas what happens when one is twenty, as I remember it, happens forever. I have not been twenty for a long time! The sun rolls toward the north and I feel, gratefully, its brightness flaming up once more. Somewhere in the world the misery we can do nothing about yet goes on. Somewhere the words I will write down next year, and the next, are drifting into the wind, out of the ornate pods of the weeds of the Provincelands.

Once I went into the woods to find an almost unfindable bird, a blue grosbeak. And I found it: a rough, deep blue, almost black, with heavy beak; it was plucking one by one the humped, pale green caterpillars from the leaves of a thick green tree. Then it vanished into the shadows of the leaves and, in the same moment, from the crown of the tree flew a western bluebird—little aqua thrush of the mountains, hundreds of miles from its home. It is a moment hard to top—but, I can. Once I came upon two angels, they were standing quietly, keeping guard beside a car. Light streamed from them, and a splash of flames lay quietly under their feet. What is one to do with such moments, such memories, but cherish them? Who knows what is beyond the known? And if you think that any day the secret of light might come, would you not keep the house of your mind ready? Would you not cleanse your study of all that is cheap, or trivial? Would you not live in continual hope, and pleasure, and excitement?

Now the green ocean begins to take on the hue and cry of its sheets of spring blue. Weary and sleepy, winter slowly polishes the moon through the long nights, then recedes to the north, its body thinning and melting, like a bundle of old riddles left, one more year, unanswered.

ACKNOWLEDGMENTS

I thank the editors of the following magazines and anthologies
in which some of these poems and essays have been printed:

Appalachia, a section of Winter Hours
Green Mountains Review, Moss
Ohio Review, Sister Turtle, and The Bright Eyes of Eleonora:
     Poe's Dream of Recapturing the Impossible
Poetry, The Storm
Poetry East, The Swan (essay)
Shenandoah, Building the House
Virginia Quarterly Review, Three Prose Poems

Sister Turtle also appears in *The Anchor Essay Annual: The Best
     of 1998,* published by Anchor Books/Doubleday.
Building the House also appears in *The Best American Essays
     1998,* published by Houghton Mifflin.
The Swan (poem) appears in my book *House of Light.* Copy-
     right © 1990 by Mary Oliver. Reprinted by permission of
     Beacon Press, Boston.